Sixteenth edition

Taking the Mystery Out of

Illinois School Finance

Thomas A. Kersten

ICPEL Publications

International Council of Professors of

Educational Leadership

Ypsilanti, Michigan

Published by ICPEL Publications, the publications arm of the International Council of Professors of Educational Leadership (ICPEL) www.icpel.org

Printed in United States of America

Library of Congress Cataloging-in-Publication Data

Kersten, Thomas A.
Taking the mystery out of Illinois school finance
ISBN 978-1-7923-1900-6(pbk)

How to order this book:

ICPEL Publications offers *Taking the Mystery Out of Illinois School Finance* as a Print-on-Demand hard copy at: www.icpel.org Books are prepared in Perfect Bound binding and delivery is 3-5 days.

Taking the Mystery Out of Illinois School Finance has been peer reviewed, accepted, and endorsed by the International Council of Professors of Educational Leadership as a significant contribution to the preparation and practice of school administration.

ICPEL Publications Director, Brad E. Bizzell
ICPEL Founding Publications Director, Theodore B. Creighton
Cover Design by Brad E. Bizzell
Cover Photography credit to Skokie School District 69

Contents

Acknowledgments

I would like to acknowledge four important individuals whose assistance was critical in helping me take the complex topic of Illinois school finance and make it much more understandable for those with limited school finance knowledge and experience.

Most of all I want to thank my wife Beth, Assistant Superintendent for Business Services in Skokie School District 68, for not only her patience and support throughout the writing process but also the invaluable background knowledge and critical assistance she provided through countless hours of conversation, editing, and revision.

Also, I want to acknowledge my good friend and former superintendent colleague, Dr. Nelson Armour, whose ongoing review and support helped shape the focus and content of this book. In addition, I want to recognize Dr. Bill Phillips, Associate Professor, at the University of Illinois at Springfield, for his assistance with the chapter on borrowing. Finally, I want to offer a special thanks to Elizabeth Hennssey, Managing Director, Raymond James & Associates, Inc., Director of Public Finance/Debt Investment Banking, for sharing her unique expertise.

Special thanks to Theodore Creighton, ICPEL Publications Founding Director and Brad Bizzell, ICPEL Publications Director.

Taking the Mystery Out of Illinois School Finance, 16th[t] Edition

Taking the Mystery Out of Illinois School Finance, which was first published in 2007, is annually revised to reflect the most up-to-date information on Illinois school finance available. As such, it provides school administrators, school board members, professors, graduate students, and other stakeholders with an easy to understand explanation of school funding. What makes this book so unique is that it is the only comprehensive Illinois school finance resource readily available today.

Taking the Mystery Out of Illinois School Finance, 16th Edition has been significantly updated this year. In addition to providing the latest facts, figures, and legal requirements, it has been expanded to include the latest information especially related to revenues, pension, and emerging issues.

Chapter 1

Understanding the Basic School Finance Principle

INTRODUCTION

The very mention of school finance to teachers, many school administrators, school board members, and other public school stakeholders usually conjures up images of jargon laden school district presentations, complicated reports, or graduate school textbooks, which seem designed to make anyone except school business officials feel confused and inadequate. For most people, school finance appears to be a quagmire of complex terms, formulas, and difficult to understand state and federal laws that are somehow inexplicably linked to both state and local politics.

To appreciate this point, consider this. Just show someone a copy of your most recent property tax bill and ask them to explain the state equalizer or the difference between assessed and equalized assessed valuation. You are likely to receive a blank stare. If you really want to confuse someone, just point to the drop in their local school district tax rate on their tax bill from last year and ask them to explain how the school portion of their property taxes increased. Too often school finance is presented just this way even to graduate students in Master of Arts programs in educational leadership. Given this traditional approach, is it any wonder that most educators find school finance very confusing?

Several years ago, a school board member in the school district where I was superintendent suggested an ingenious test to judge how clearly we were communicating with our stakeholders. We ultimately named it the 7-Eleven Test. It was simultaneously a complex yet simple way to judge whether we were effective communicators. The premise behind the 7-Eleven Test is this. No matter what educational program or issue you have, you should be able to walk down to your local 7-Eleven and explain it in such a way that anyone in the store can understand you.

One of the communication problems we often have as school administrators, especially in the area of school district finances, is that we have not emphasized the 7-Eleven Test enough. In fact, most of the time when we discuss school finance, we do so in such excessive educational jargon and excruciating detail that even many school administrators cannot comprehend it.

This book, *Taking the Mystery Out of Illinois School Finance*, is written with the 7-Eleven Test in mind. It is designed to explain the key principles of Illinois school finance in a way that graduate students, teachers, school board members, parents, building-level school administrators, and other interested citizens can grasp the essential content without getting bogged down in excessive financial detail. Only by understanding the basics of Illinois school finance, can school administrators, board members, and other constituents make informed decisions.

THE CENTRAL THEME – REVENUES VERSUS EXPENDITURES

The general principle behind school finance is actually quite simple. In its most basic form, school finance is a two-sided equation with revenues on one side and expenditures on the other. If revenues meet or exceed expenses regularly, your school district is financially solvent. However, when expenses start to exceed revenues, particularly over multiple years, the school district is probably heading toward financial difficulty, sometimes even if it has a large cash reserve.

A good way to understand this basic principle is to relate school finances to personal finances. Let's assume that you earn $50,000 per year. If your expenses are below $50,000 annually and expected to remain so for the foreseeable future, you are financially solvent. That is, you have more income than you need. However, if you begin to see that your expenses are growing faster than your salary and you have to dip into your savings to pay your monthly bills, you are now in deficit spending. Your personal finances, in this instance, parallel those of school districts. If school district revenues exceed expenditures year after year, the district is quite solvent. However, once their expenditures begin exceeding revenues on a regular basis, the district too has a deficit problem.

As an individual you have, of course, several realistic options to eliminate your personal deficit. First, you could cut your expenses. This approach, however, may mean that you cannot do some of the things to which you have become accustomed. You may have to go out to dinner less often, postpone a vacation, or keep your present car a few years longer. You could also look for a new position with a higher salary or consider supplementing your income by taking a part-time job. Some combination of these strategies may solve your personal deficit spending problem.

School districts, on the other hand, have a very similar problem but without many of the options available to you. Similar to your personal finances, when school district revenues fail to keep up with expenditures, school administrators and school boards must increase revenues and/or cut expenditures. They will need to use their cash reserves just as you might tap into your savings account to cover immediate shortfalls.

Chapter 1

As you will see shortly, the most significant difference between individuals and school districts is that school districts have fewer options primarily on the revenue side to solve their financial problems than do individuals. Also, school boards must conduct their business in public view while subject, at times, to an uninformed and sometimes angry public and special interest groups. The political nature of school governance at the state and school board levels is a challenge that individuals do not typically face. Yet, once you understand the basic revenue/expenditure principle of state and local school district finances, much of the mystery of school finance will disappear.

Chapter 2

Historical Basis for Public School Funding

Before considering school district finances, it is important to understand why the federal government plays such a small role in public education. It is equally important to understand what role it does play. Let's begin with some questions.

- Do you know why state legislators, rather the federal government, seem so much more involved in public education?
- Have you ever lived in another state with just a handful of county-wide school districts and wondered why some states such as Illinois have hundreds of school districts, some with as few as a hundred or two hundred students?
- Have you noticed that certain states have had their funding systems ruled unconstitutional while a state such as Illinois with a tremendous variance in the amount spent per pupil between the wealthy and poorer school districts is allowed to continue as is?

The answer to these central questions requires a very basic understanding of the legal authority for public education.

LEGAL AUTHORITY FOR PUBLIC EDUCATION

Shortly after this country was founded, the U. S. Constitution was written establishing the legal authority for public education. The key section was the tenth amendment which states that, "The powers not delegated to the United States by the Constitution, nor prohibited by it to the States, are reserved to the States, or to the people." (Yudof, Kirp & Levin, 1992, p. 841). Through this amendment, our founding fathers delegated to the states, not the federal government, the legal authority for the governance of public education. Ultimately, states created their own unique public education systems through their individual state constitutions. As a result, even though public education systems are similar from state to state, the delegation of the responsibility for public education to the states has meant that each is at liberty to design its own public education system within the parameters of federal law.

Does this mean that the federal government has no role in public education? Far from it. Although the federal government does not have direct control over public education, it is not without influence. However, because of the tenth amendment, its influence has historically been less than that of state government.

ROLE OF THE FEDERAL GOVERNMENT

Since the federal government has no direct authority for public education, its primary mode of action is to pass legislation often linked directly to federal funding. In essence, national political leaders create public policy by tying initiatives to federal dollars. States and more specifically school districts that want federal funding are required to meet certain federal requirements. This formula approach has proven to be a particularly effective way for federal policy-makers to influence public education on a national level.

KEY FEDERAL INITIATIVES

To further understand how the federal government influences public education, let's take a brief look at four historic federal educational initiatives. Although a discussion of all federal initiatives is impractical and unnecessary, understanding these which have substantially impacted the development of American public education and to some degree educational funding will provide valuable insights into how the federal government uses dollars to influence public education policy and programming.

LAND ORDINANCE OF 1785

A landmark piece of federal legislation, the Land Ordinance of 1785, is one of these initiatives (Brimley & Garfield, 2002). Adopted by the Continental Congress on May 20, 1785, it had several purposes; however, one of its key provisions was to divide the land acquired from Britain following the Revolutionary War, primarily in the Midwest, into six mile square townships, each composed of 36 one square mile blocks (See Table 2.1 below). Depending upon natural factors such as rivers, the size of the actual township could vary. The federal government then sold many of these sections to raise capital, in part, to repay war debt. However, a unique provision of the Act was the requirement that Section 16 of the thirty-six mile square block be set aside for the maintenance of public schools. Many of these were sold to raise revenue for public education. Additional land ordinance legislation called the Northwest Ordinance was passed in 1787. It included the phrase, "…religion, morality, and knowledge being necessary to good government and the happiness of mankind, schools and the means of school shall be forever encouraged." This gave further impetus to establishing a priority for public education in areas beyond the original thirteen states and also a property basis for school funding (Alexander & Alexander, 2005, p.1019).

Table 2.1
Township Grid

1	2	3	4	5	6
7	8	9	10	11	12
13	14	15	16	17	18
19	20	21	22	13	24
25	26	27	28	29	30
31	32	33	34	35	36

Think for a moment how this Act is reflected in Illinois even today. As an Illinois resident, you can probably identify the township in which you live. If not, you will likely find the township listed on your property tax bill. To understand how the township system still impacts Illinois public schools, let us use Niles Township as an example. The township is composed of the following elementary (K-8) school districts:

- Golf School District 67
- Skokie School District 68
- Skokie School District 69
- Morton Grove School District 70
- Niles School District 71
- Fairview School District 72
- East Prairie School District 73
- Skokie School District 73 ½
- Lincolnwood School District 74

With the exception of a small portion of Golf 67 that was annexed to Glenview Consolidated School District 34 in the 1980s, all school district boundaries are coterminous (same boundaries) with Niles Township High School District 219, which is the public high school district serving all township students. You may note the use of the term township in the name of the high school district.

This township pattern is common in Illinois, although outside the suburban Chicago area, many school districts are actually unit (K-12) districts. Over the years, various school district consolidation efforts and other factors have altered the original pattern in some areas of the state. However, the importance of the Land Ordinance of 1785 on the growth and funding of public schools cannot be underestimated.

FEDERAL VOCATIONAL EDUCATION ACT

In 1917, federal legislation entitled the Federal Vocational Education Act, sometimes referred to as the Smith-Hughes Act, became law. For the first time, federal funds were used to support the development of pre-collegiate courses in vocational education and related teacher training. By earmarking these funds, the federal government supported the development of public school vocational education programs throughout the country (Guthrie, 2003). This is a good example of how the federal government uses dollars to promote a specific educational initiative without the legal authority to mandate it.

ELEMENTARY AND SECONDARY EDUCATION ACT OF 1965 (ESEA)

A more recent and sweeping example of a federal policy is the Elementary and Secondary Education Act of 1965 which was originally signed into law by President Lyndon B. Johnson in 1965. A central component of Johnson's War on Poverty, ESEA was designed to assist primarily economically disadvantaged students through funding a variety of federal programs. ESEA was divided into various sections called Titles. One of the most well known was Title I: Improving the Academic Achievement of the Disadvantaged. Title I, a federal grant program, was created to improve the reading and mathematics achievement of children from lower socioeconomic backgrounds. School districts seeking federal Title I funding must provide certain types of student services and follow grant guidelines to be eligible. Most school districts continue to receive federal Title I dollars even today (Beyer & Johnson, 2005).

Since 1965, ESEA has been periodically reauthorized, each time reflecting the educational policy agenda of the federal government at the time. Under the Bush administration, it was reauthorized a s No Child Left Behind (Beyer & Johnson, 2005). The most recent reauthorization under the Obama administration was the Every Student Succeeds Act. Since the Obama presidency, ESEA has received very little attention. What remains are the Title program grants.

EDUCATION OF ALL HANDICAPPED CHILDREN ACT OF 1975 (PUBLIC LAW 94-142)

One of my most vivid teaching memories from the early 1970s is trying to teach language arts in an affluent suburban Chicago school district in heterogeneous classes of twenty-five plus students. In each class, I had some students who were academically gifted and a few who could barely read and write beyond a primary grade level. As an English major trained primarily in the greatest works of literature, I had very little preparation to teach low functioning students in my language arts class. As a beginning teacher, I decided to approach our school counselors for advice. I assumed that either they would be able to provide me with advice or recommend a veteran teacher who could mentor me.

After I explained the difficulties I was having and asked for advice, I remember how the counselor, a very experienced faculty member, leaned back in his desk chair while smoking his pipe and offered me his sage advice. He began by saying that there are just some students who are like this. He said that he did not have any specific suggestions other than to do the best I could with these children. I was amazed by his comments. Surely, another faculty member must have had success with needy students. As I asked other teachers, I received the same advice.

What I realized later was that special education was in its infancy. Our school, which was in a very progressive district, had only one Educationally Mentally Handicapped (EMH) classroom and two resource tutors who periodically pulled students from class for individual reading support. I remember a year later hearing about an area special education cooperative but knew almost nothing about it. So was the state of special education in the early '70s.

Then along came PL 94-142, Educational of all Handicapped Children Act. The passage of this federal legislation guaranteed for the first time a free, appropriate public education to each child with disabilities (United States Office of Special Education Programs, 2023). The rest, of course, is history. Beginning with this federal legislation which includes funding support, the growth of special education programs and services has been dramatic. Today this is probably the most far reaching and extensive federal policy initiative impacting public education.

SUMMARY

In Chapter 2, we examined the legal basis for our system of public education including the impact of the 10th amendment. We also studied four examples of historic federal legislation to understand how the federal government uses its resources to influence people's lives through public education policy and programming even without direct constitutional authority.

Chapter 3

Sources of Revenue

Now that we have taken a brief look at the legal basis for public education and examined the role of the federal government, let us turn our attention to the first side of the basic finance equation – sources of revenue; or more specifically, where school districts find the dollars to operate. Overall, school districts rely on several primary revenue sources including:

- Property taxes;
- General State Aid;
- Poverty Grant;
- Categorical State Aid;
- Competitive grants;
- Corporate Personal Property Replacement Tax (CPPRT);
- Federal aid;
- Local fees; and,
- Interest income.

PROPERTY TAXES

I am sure that you would not be surprised to hear that the largest single source of Illinois public education funding is the property tax. In fact, in fiscal year 2021, local sources of revenue, which are primarily property taxes, comprised 43.5% of all public school revenues in Illinois (Illinois State Board of Education, 2022a). Note: In school finance, fiscal year refers to a traditional school year July 1 to June 30. Therefore, FY 24 is July 1, 2023 through June 30, 2024. For some school districts, primarily in the northeast portion of the state, property taxes are the most substantial revenue source accounting for more than half of their total revenues. However, for other school districts with lower property tax bases, the impact of property taxes may be somewhat less than other revenue sources since their property tax bases provide a smaller portion of overall school district revenues. Also not surprising, some districts with low property wealth, such as those in rural areas, experience little if any property value growth from year to year.

TAX BASE

A school district's wealth is usually linked to the total value of taxable property within district boundaries. This is what is called the tax base. A school district's tax base is determined by adding together the value of all taxable property whether it is vacant land, residential, or business-based. Since the value of property varies depending on its location and type, some school districts will have much more property wealth than others.

For example, if your school district is located in the northern suburbs of Chicago and includes a regional shopping mall and multiple high-rise corporate office buildings, your overall tax base will be dramatically higher than in a farming community in Livingston County. Because of such wide discrepancies in Illinois school district tax bases, a great deal of inequity exists between the highest and lowest wealth school districts.

TAX EXEMPT PROPERTY

Some property owners do not pay property taxes because the property is tax exempt. Examples of common tax exempt properties include those occupied by governmental units such as military bases, municipal and state offices, and legally designated not-for-profits such as places of worship, some hospitals, universities, and other organizations. For many school districts, tax exempt properties are a small percentage of the overall tax base. But in others, such as Evanston Community Consolidated School District 65, which includes Northwestern University, a significant portion of property is not taxed and is unavailable for other development thereby reducing the school district's property tax base.

UNDERSTANDING THE PROPERTY TAX IN ILLINOIS

Before considering issues surrounding property taxes, it is important to understand how property taxes are calculated. Theoretically, calculations for all taxable property in Illinois should, by law, be based on one-third of the property's market value (actual selling price) (Illinois Department of Revenue, 2023c). Therefore, if your home has a market value of $600,000, it should be assessed for tax calculation purposes at 1/3 or $200,000. This $200,000 is called the assessed valuation. All Illinois counties including Cook are supposed to tax property based on one-third of market value. However, here is where Cook County differs from the rest of the state. Cook County, instead of assessing all property at 33%, uses a tiered system, which assesses business property at a higher rate than residential property.

Let's examine this a little closer. In Cook County, homeowners' property should be assessed at 16% of market value and businesses between 33% and 38%, depending upon the type of business entity (Illinois Department of Revenue, 2023c). However, beginning with 2009 taxes received in 2010, Cook County residential property will be assessed at ten percent and commercial property at twenty-five percent (Houlihan, 2009).

In all other counties, both homeowners and businesses are assessed at 33%. The figure below shows the legal assessment percentages.

Table 3.1
County Tax Assessment Levels

Tax Payer	Cook County	Other Counties
Homeowner	10%	33%
Businesses	25%	33%

This multi-tiered assessment system in Cook County was designed to reduce homeowner property taxes. In essence, businesses pay a higher percentage of the overall taxes to allow homeowners to pay less.

The concept of fixed assessment levels for property tax purposes seems logical and fair. If all Illinois real estate was assessed according to the mandated formula, the system would appear to be fair since everyone would be treated consistently. However, have you ever compared your tax bill with a neighbor, perhaps even with someone who has the same model home in your subdivision, and wondered why that person's tax bill was different from yours? If so, you are not alone.

PROPERTY ASSESSMENT INCONSISTENCIES

To understand why this occurs, it is important to recognize that assessment of property is not an exact science. In Illinois, county property tax assessors oversee the assessment and reassessment of all property in their respective counties. As with any such process, the assessment process is somewhat subjective since it relies on individuals who have some discretion to interpret information and make judgments. As a result, property assessments vary from area to area from year to year.

In addition, Cook County property has been historically under-assessed. However, state law allows Cook County to establish different assessment levels for various classes of property, of which there are currently 13 (Illinois Department of Revenue, 2023c). As a result, of these underassessment practices, the Cook County Board revised the Real Property Assessment Classification Ordinance to set residential assessment at 10% and business/commercial at 25% beginning with 2009 assessments (Herman & Kownacki, 2008).

To adjust for some of the assessment variance from county to county, the state created a balancing system called the State Equalization Factor.

STATE EQUALIZATION FACTOR

The State Equalization Factor or as it is commonly called the "Multiplier" is a factor assigned to a county to bring the average county-wide property assessment level to the required one-third (Illinois Department of Revenue, 2023c). If a county is under-assessing, the state can eliminate some of the discrepancy by increasing the multiplier.

Here is how it works. When property in a given county is correctly assessed at one-third of its market value, the state assigns a multiplier of 1.0. On the other hand, when property in a county is under-assessed, the state assigns the county a higher multiplier, which is applied equally to all property in the county. The multiplier is supposed to bring the overall assessment of property in the county to the one-third standard. For example, the state assigned a multiplier of 3.0027 for Cook County for 2021 because both residential and business/commercial properties were under assessed (Illinois Department of Revenue, 2023d).

The table below demonstrates the different assessment levels in Cook and Lake Counties. It also shows how the multiplier is used to bring property assessments to the mandated level. You will note that businesses in Cook are assessed at a significantly higher than residential property. Also, by applying the multiplier, the state has attempted to bring the total county-wide property assessment in Cook to 33% of the total market value.

Table 3.2
Effect of Multiplier

County	Market Value	Assessed Value	Multiplier	*Equalized Assessed Value*
Lake-Home	$600,000	$200,000	1	$200,000
Lake-Business	$600,000	$200,000	1	$200,000
Cook-Home	$600,000	$60,000	3.0027	$180,162
Cook-Business	$600,000	$150,000	3.0027	$450,405

EQUALIZED ASSESSED VALUATION (EAV)

In the figure above, you may have noticed that I introduced a new term, Equalized Assessed Valuation (EAV). Since assessment levels may vary from county to county, in particular from Cook, the property tax calculation you will see shortly requires that assessed values be converted to EAV as part of the property tax calculation process. So when you hear EAV, be aware that this is the revised assessed value of the home after the state multiplier has been applied to adjust for under-assessment.

FURTHER EXEMPTIONS

If calculating property taxes was not complicated enough, the state legislature has created several special tax exemptions designed to reduce property taxes for specific groups (Illinois Department of Revenue, 2023c). These "exempt" a portion of the EAV from the property tax calculation thereby reducing taxes for that particular property. The most common exemptions in Illinois are:

- Homestead (An exemption for owners of primary residences);
- Senior Homestead (Additional exemption for seniors); and,
- Disabled Veterans.

In addition, low income seniors who meet certain eligibility requirements qualify for a Senior Citizen Assessment Freeze. Later in this chapter, we will examine a sample property tax bill which will include some of these exemptions.

So far, we have discussed several factors which are used in the property tax calculation: market value, assessed valuation, equalized assessed valuation (EAV), and exemptions. The last factor you need to understand is tax rate.

TAX RATE

The most confusing term in the property tax formula is the tax rate, which is the percentage at which property is taxed. State laws regulate tax rates. However, for most individuals other than school business officials and superintendents, what is most important to know is not how the tax rate is calculated but rather how it is applied to individual taxpayer bills. Since the imposition of the tax cap in Illinois and recent legislation, the tax rate has become a less important factor for school districts. Tax rate will be discussed further later.

PROPERTY TAX FORMULA

Now that we have examined the factors that are used in the property tax calculation, we can now apply the formula. Although the mathematical calculation is quite simple, it often appears confusing unless you understand the factors. I like to tell graduate students that the actual math problem could easily be completed by many third graders! What makes the formula particularly confusing is that the tax rate is applied for every one hundred dollars of EAV not total EAV. The property tax formula is:

- Individual Property Owner's EAV/100 X Total Tax Rate = Total Property Tax Bill
- To understand this calculation, let's consider a specific example of a typical home. Our assumptions are:
  (a) Home has an EAV of $50,000 (Market value of $150,000) and
  (b) The total tax rate for all taxing bodies is $6.00.

Here is the calculation:

Step 1: Take the EAV and divide it by 100. The formula says that the tax rate is applied to every $100 of EAV not the total amount. Therefore, you must calculate how many hundreds of dollars of EAV you have.

$50,000/100 = $500

Step 2: Multiple this number by the tax rate. In reality, the property owner is paying $6.00 in property taxes on every 100 of EAV.

$500 X $6.00 = $3,000

It is that simple! What confuses everyone is how you arrive at the tax rate and how you calculate the final EAV.

UNDERSTANDING A TAX BILL

Have you ever studied your own property tax bill? You have probably looked at the bottom line, compared various figures from the current to last year's but never really took time to understand it. Yet, one of the best ways to understand property taxes is to examine an actual property tax bill. The basic components of property tax bills are common in all counties. However, because Cook County is different in some respects, we will examine a sample Cook County tax bill (See Sample Cook County Tax Bill below).

To begin, you will note that this is the second installment, which is due in the fall. In the bottom left-hand corner, you will find the amount paid in the first installment, $9,146.82, and second, $7,580.96. The total property taxes due on this residential property for the year are $16,727.78.

COOK COUNTY TAX CALCULATION

This bill illustrates how Cook County property taxes are billed differently from the remainder of the state. This taxpayer paid a first installment of $9,146.82 for tax year 2021 in spring 2022, which was 55% of the previous year's total bill. Since the first installment is due earlier in Cook than other counties, the exact annual property tax is unknown at the time so 55% of the prior year's amount is billed. The second installment is $7, 580.96, which reflects the difference between the first installment and the total actual property taxes due after property tax calculations are completed.

2021 Second Installment Property Tax Bill

I1356/ 1 oi I M

TOTAL PAYMENT DUE	
$ 7,580.96	
By 12/30/22 (on time)	

Property Index Number (PIN)	Volume	Code	Tax Year	(Payable In)	Township	Classification
		)38	2021	2022	NORTHFIELD	2-78

IF PAYING LATE, PLEASE PAY	12/31/22 - 02/01/23 $7,694.67	OR 02/02/23 - 03/01/23 $7,808.38	OR 03/02/23 - 04/01/23 $7,922.09	LATE INTEREST IS 1.5% PER MONTH, BY STATE LAW

TAXING DISTRICT BREAKDOWN

Taxing District	2021 Tax	2021 Rate	2021 %	Pension	2020 Tax
MISCELLANEOUS TAXES					
North Shore Mosq Abate. Dist Northfield	18.16	0.009	0.11%		19.62
Metro Water Reclamation Dist of Chicago	770.90	0.382	4.61%	84.75	823.90
Glenview Park District	1,325.87	0.657	7.93%	108.97	1,288.16
Miscellaneous Taxes Total	2,114.93	1.048	12.65%		2,131.68
SCHOOL TAXES					
Oakton College Dist Skokie Des Plaines	508.55	0.252	3.04%		494.78
Glenbrook HS District 225 (Glenview)	4,661.74	2.310	27.87%	163.46	4,542.35
School District CC 34	6,508.28	3.225	38.91%	167.49	6,508.38
School Taxes Total	11,678.57	5.787	69.82%		11,545.51
MUNICIPALITY/TOWNSHIP TAXES					
Glenview Library Fund	676.05	0.335	4.04%		664.79
Village of Glenview	1,025.18	0.508	6.13%	653.85	1,004.81
Road & Bridge Northfield	110.99	0.055	0.66%		106.80
General Assistance Northfield	16.14	0.008	0.10%		15.26
Town of Northfield	50.45	0.025	0.30%		47.95
Municipality/Township Taxes Total	1,878.81	0.931	11.23%		1,839.61
COOK COUNTY TAXES					
Cook County Forest Preserve District	117.05	0.058	0.70%	4.03	126.42
Consolidated Elections	38.34	0.019	0.23%		0.00
County of Cook	490.41	0.243	2.92%	177.59	592.85
Cook County Public Safety	264.37	0.131	1.58%		287.71
Cook County Health Facilities	145.30	0.072	0.87%		106.80
Cook County Taxes Total	1,055.47	0.523	6.30%		1,113.78
(Do not pay these totals)	16,727.78	8.289	100.00%		16,630.58

TAX CALCULATOR

2020 Assessed Value	73,203
2021 Property Value	732,030
2021 Assessment Level X	10%
2021 Assessed Value	73,203
2021 State Equalizer X	3.0027
2021 Equalized Assessed Value (EAV)	219,807
2021 Local Tax Rate X	8.289%
2021 Total Tax Before Exemptions	18,219.80

2021 Total Tax Before Exemptions 18,219.80
Homeowner's Exemption -828.90
Senior Citizen Exemption -663.12
Senior Freeze Exemption .00
2021 Total Tax After Exemptions 16,727.78
First Installment 9,146.82
Second Installment + 7,580.96
Total 2021 Tax (Payable in 2022) 16,727.78

IMPORTANT MESSAGES

PROPERTY LOCATION | MAILING ADDRESS

GLENVIEW IL 60025-7611

DETACH & INCLUDE WITH PAYMENT

Figure 3.1. Sample Cook County Tax Bill

YEAR IN ARREARS

When you hear that property taxes are always billed a year behind, this is because they are assessed in one year, in this case 2021, and actually paid in the next, 2022. This bill provides an example of this process, which often causes some confusion when trying to explain property taxes.

Adding further to possible misinterpretation is the difference between tax year and the fiscal year. In the Sample Tax Bill above, the tax year is January 1 to December 31 and is different from fiscal year which is always July 1 to June 30.

REASSESSMENT PRACTICES

The 2020 Assessed Value is $73,203. This can remain the same from one year to the next if it is not a reassessment year. Cook County property is reassessed every three years.

In other counties, state statute requires that individual properties be reviewed every four years. However, it is common for townships in these counties to review the fair market value of properties annually against assessment levels, sometimes resulting in the application of a township equalizer.

TAXING DISTRICTS

The tax bill also identifies the taxing bodies legally authorized to levy property taxes. On the sample bill, both the elementary and high school districts collect the majority of property taxes. One interesting point to remember is that taxing bodies are not required to levy taxes. In non-election years, for example, no taxes are typically collected for "Consolidated Elections."

TAX RATES

As mentioned earlier, tax rates are very confusing particularly since the property tax cap became law in such counties as Cook. What actually occurs is that the tax rate is calculated after the amount of property taxes a district is entitled to under law is determined and the overall EAV within the boundaries of the taxing body is established. The tax rate is then set at the level needed to generate the amount of property taxes the taxing body is requesting as long as the rate does not exceed the maximum permitted by law. If it does, then the tax rate is reduced to the legal limit (3.50 in Education Fund) and the taxing body does not receive all the property taxes requested. This is one of the reasons that school districts ask the voters to approve a tax increase through a referendum.

TAX CALCULATOR

Earlier we discussed the formula used to calculate a property owner's tax liability. In summary, the EAV of the property is divided by 100 and multiplied by the tax rate to establish the total property taxes due for the year. You can understand this process by examining the information listed under Tax Calculator on right side of the sample tax bill.

2020 Assessed Value. This represents the value assigned to the property by the county assessor for the prior tax year.

2021 Property Value. This line should be the projected value of the home if it was sold.

2021 Assessed Value. This figure represents the assessed value based on the county assessor's calculation for this tax year. If you simple multiple the property value, $732,203, by 10%, you have an assessed value of $73,203.

2021 State Equalization Factor. By law, the combined assessed value of all property in the county must be 33% of the actual value. Because the assessment system used by the Cook County Assessor results in a total assessment that is much lower than 33%, the state assigns a "multiplier" to bring the total assessed value to 33% in an attempt to equalize low assessed values. Since the state has assigned the county a multiplier of 3.0027, the property was substantially under assessed in relation to other counties.

2021 Tax Rate and 2021 Total Tax before Exemptions. Now that the EAV is set, the actual tax calculation can occur. The County Clerk divides the EAV, $219,807 by 100, which equals $2,198.07 and then multiplies this figure by the tax rate of 8.289, which yields a Tax Year 2021 (payable in 2022) bill of $18,219.80.

Tax Exemption. In Illinois, certain taxpayers are provided some property tax relief through the legislative process. This particular homeowner received a Homeowner's Exemption of $828.90. Most homeowners have a Homeowners Exemption and receive a reduction in property taxes due to a reduction made in the EAV. This taxpayer also received a Senior Exemption of $663.12.

2021 Total Tax after Exemptions. To arrive at the final property tax bill, the homeowner exemption amount is deducted from the amount listed under Property Tax before Exemptions, which determines the total property taxes paid in 2022. For this property, this was $16,727.78.

In other counties, the homeowner exemption may be stated as an amount of EAV, which is deducted from the total EAV rather than a dollar amount. In any event, they both reduce the taxpayer's property taxes.

What never ceases to amaze me is just how complicated the formula appears to be. However, when you understand each of the parts, the actual calculation is quite simple. The real challenge for school administrators and school board members is to explain this process to citizens and employees in a way that they understand the calculation but also appreciate the issues and political factors which have and continue to play a role in this process over time, particularly since any major revision is not imminent.

TAX COLLECTION TIMELINE

School districts submit their property tax levy to the county by the last Tuesday in December. The tax levy is the specific dollar amount in property taxes that the school district requests. We will examine further how the levy is determined when we discuss the Illinois tax cap.

Property taxes are collected twice a year and distributed to taxing bodies as they are received. School districts typically receive their first property tax payments in the spring. Since these arrive before the beginning of the school year for which they are intended, they are referred to as early taxes.

Early taxes can be a source of confusion for some school districts. For example, if your district is in the process of contract negotiations and receives $3,000,000 in early taxes, the teachers' union may argue that the district has an additional $3,000,000 in reserves. The school board may counter that this is not part of the carryover reserve, but only a temporary increase in the reserve because the funds are actually for the next school year.

One other confusing property tax issue is how Cook County residential spring property tax bills are calculated. School districts have to request property taxes in December before they know how much they are entitled to receive. The county clerk's office determines the exact level later in the spring. Because Cook County tax bills are distributed before the process is completed, the Cook County Clerk bills the property owner for 55% of the last year's tax. Then, in the fall after all pertinent data have been received, the actual full-year tax bill is calculated. The difference between what the property owner paid in the first installment and what is outstanding is the amount the property owner is billed for the fall installment. This is why the second half property tax bill may be higher or lower than the first. Since other counties distribute the first tax bill later than in Cook, usually in June, this is not an issue for the counties as the total property tax bill is divided equally between the two payments.

EVIDENCE-BASED FUNDING (FORMERLY GENERAL STATE AID)

In Illinois, 2017 was truly a landmark year in public school funding as a new state aid formula was passed by the legislature signed into law by the governor. For the first time in many years, a legislative agreement was reached to shift from a foundation level-based model to a new formula, the Evidence-Based Model (EBM). Prior to this change, Illinois was widely recognized as having one of the most regressive and inequitable state education funding systems in the country. Students who most needed support received the least. Consequently, the EBM was designed to address the large funding inequities between the wealthiest and poorest school districts in the state.

EVIDENCE-BASED MODEL

The EBM was created to close this equity gap between poorer and wealthier school districts, while taking into account the unique needs of certain at-risk student groups such as low income, special education, and bilingual students. The goal is to close the gap and ensure it remains closed. It is also designed to ensure that all students receive adequate funding support regardless of socioeconomic need. The hope is that EBM will provide a long-term funding fix.

Under the prior funding system, a substantial portion of state school funding was provided regardless of local school district wealth. Because wealthier school districts had strong property tax bases, they were better positioned to provide more programs and services than poorer school districts.

The EBM re-designed how Illinois public schools will be funded from the state moving forward. Fundamental to the EBM formula are four goals.
- Ensure that student needs are the basis for funding;
- Ensure that state funding dollars are primarily directed to the least wealthy school districts;
- Ensure that all school districts receive at least their current level of funding; and,
- Reduce the reliance on property taxes while matching the district's taxing effort to its ability to pay (Fix the Formula Illinois, 2017).

To accomplish these goals, 27 evidence-based practices or essential elements are tied to the new funding formula (Illinois Association of School Administrators, 2017). These were selected because research studies have shown that each is significantly related to increased student achievement. These elements fall into several broad categories including:
- Class size ratios;
- Specialist, support staff, and school administration staffing;
- Teacher training;
- Dollars spent for instructional materials, assessment, technology, and student activities;
- Central district services provided; and,
- Needs of diverse learners.

In order to ensure that research-based elements remain up-to-date, the new model includes a provision for a Professional Judgment Panel to review the formula periodically. Members consist of state educators as well as members from the State Board of Education, state educational associations, and the General Assembly. The Panel will meet annually to review the average of all element expenses and recommend any changes in the formula, which members deem necessary in order to maintain a funding system consistent with the four key goals (Fix the Formula Illinois, 2017).

The EBM consists of four major components: adequacy target, capacity target, percent of adequacy, and distribution method. Each of these is described below.

Adequacy Target

The initial step in the model's implementation is determining the adequacy target. This is the district specific level of funding needed to provide a high-quality education to each district/student. Using the essential elements and the actual per-pupil cost of meeting these elements, an adequacy target is calculated for each school district. This amount is adjusted by employee cost differences in various regions of the state.

Local Capacity Target

After determining the adequacy target, a local capacity target, which is the amount a district can contribute to reaching its adequacy target, is calculated. It is defined as the amount the district can contribute toward meeting the adequacy target and is largely made up of local property taxes and corporate personnel property tax receipts as well as EBM funding.

Percent of Adequacy

The next step in the process is to calculate how well funded the district is from local sources relative to its adequacy target. Factors used to determine this percent include local capacity and current state funding. Once a percentage of adequacy is calculated, the school district can then be placed in a tier to determine the amount of new money it will receive.

Distribution Method

The final step is determining how new/additional state funds will be distributed to school districts. Under the EBM, new state dollars are directed to those districts with the lowest percent of adequacy met. However, the distribution method defines how new dollars are directed to all school districts. To distribute new state dollars, all school districts are placed in one of four tiers based upon their adequacy target percentage. These are defined below.

- Tier 1: These are the poorest school districts. Fifty percent of all new dollars will be allocated to these school districts, which have an adequacy percentage below 50%.
- Tier 2: Those, which have an adequacy percentage below 90% including Tier 1 districts, will receive 49% of new dollars.
- Tier 3: Districts with an adequacy percentage between 90% and 100% will receive 0.9% of new dollars.
- Tier 4: Districts with adequacy levels above 100% qualify for 0.1% of new dollars.

In actuality, the distribution method is designed to raise the level of funding to the neediest school districts up to the adequacy target for each school district (i.e., all districts move closer to 100% adequacy with those farthest away receiving the most new money and moving fastest toward adequacy). Proration on a per pupil funding basis would only occur if the state provides less support than in the prior year (Illinois State Board of Education. (2023b).

Basic Funding Minimum

Under the new model, a base funding minimum guarantees that districts receive per pupil state funding at least the same level as they did the prior fiscal year. Any additional funds that districts receive through this process are included in their base funding minimum for the next year.

POVERTY GRANTS

Under the former funding system, school districts with a minimum number of low-income students receive additional state funding through the state poverty grant program. The amount of funding received was calculated under a separate statutory formula based on Illinois Department of Human Services (DHS) low income populations for benefit recipients. This included a three-year average of the unduplicated count of district students who qualified for Medicaid or food stamps. School districts with 15% or less qualifying students received a flat $355 per student. For districts over 15%, the amount of funding increased based on the percentage of qualifying students. The formula was often described as curvilinear since the rate of per pupil funding increased more as the percentage of low-income students increased in a school district (Illinois State Board of Education, 2020c).

Poverty Grant Funding, though, was not equity-based. The formula did not include consideration of local district wealth but only the low-income student count. As a result, even wealthy school districts received the same level of funding as the least wealthy if they had the same percentage of qualifying students. In fact, some school districts, especially those under the flat grant formula, may actually receive more poverty grant funding than GSA funding.

Under the EBM, poverty grant funding will remain. However, it is folded into the new model rather than distributed separately. It is also one of the risk factors taken into account under the EBM.

OTHER CHANGES

As part of the political process that led to this historic new Illinois school funding formula, several other changes affecting school finance were also approved (Fix the Formula Illinois, 2017).

Chicago Block Grant (CBG)
Any changes in how Illinois schools are funded must include Chicago School

District 299 even though in some aspects, Chicago Public Schools are funded differently from the rest of the state. Much of the difference is attributable to the Chicago Block Grant, which was created in 1995 and will remain in place under the new funding model. Unlike other Illinois districts that had to apply for certain funds, Chicago simply received a specific percentage of state funding linked to certain state budget line items. Some of these are now included in the new formula similar to other school districts. However, others such as the Early Childhood Block Grant and a special education private tuition as well as funding for transportation will still be provided separately through the new formula.

Tax Credits for Scholarships

Illinois now has a tax credit plan that allows taxpayers to donate funds for scholarships for low-income students who attend private/parochial schools. Those who donate can receive up to a 75 percent state income tax reduction for donated funds. Donors are permitted to specify individual or multiple schools for which their donations are applicable. They are not permitted to designate specific individuals or groups of students. Corporate donors are not allowed any designation options. Seventy-five million dollars has been allocated for the first year of this program. The amount will be re-evaluated annually thereafter.

The low-income family maximum is set at 300 percent of the poverty level. However, those students with a family income of 185 percent or less of the poverty level can receive 100 percent in scholarships for necessary costs and fees. Those between 185 percent and 250 per cent receive up to 75 percent, while those greater than 250 percent to 300 percent can qualify for a 50 percent scholarship.

Referendum Option for Property Tax Reduction

Another new provision is the inclusion of a process that taxpayers may follow to reduce local property taxes. If a school district is more than 110 percent above its adequacy target, taxpayers may initiate a referendum seeking to reduce school district property taxes by up to 10 percent down to the 110 percent level, but not further. Similar to the backdoor referendum process, the petitioners would need to gather a petition signed by 10 percent of registered voters for the latest election to put the question on the ballot. If approved, the tax reduction could not allow the district to fall below the 110 percent adequacy target. This provision was tested in Lisle School District 202 where it failed.

Mandate Relief

Several specific state mandate changes were also approved. Local school boards can reduce daily physical education from five to three days. They can also waive the physical education requirement for students in grades 7-12 who participate in interscholastic or extracurricular activities. Streamlined were the requirements for contracting driver's education services and the state mandate waiver process.

CATEGORICAL STATE AID

Under the EBM, categorical state aid funding has also changed. In the past, school districts annually submitted categorical grant applications in the summer and generally received quarterly payments during the year. Under the new model, four of the previous categorical grants related to at-risk indications will be folded into the evidence-based funding payment. These include:

- Special Education Personnel;
- Special Education Funding for Children;
- Special Education Summer School; and,
- Bilingual Education.

The other common categorical state areas will remain as stand-alone funded programs. These include:
- Special Education and Regular and Vocational Transportation;
- Special Education Private Tuition;
- Regular Education Orphanage;
- Driver's Education; and,
- Free Breakfast/Lunch.

These categorical state aid programs have been an important source of revenue for all school districts, even those with high levels of per pupil spending. In fact, districts previously funded under the flat grant model usually received more actual dollars per student from categorical grants than general state aid funding. At this time, it is unclear exactly how these changes to categorical funding will affect individual school districts.

IMPLICATIONS OF FUNDING CHANGES FOR ILLINOIS SCHOOL DISTRICTS

Clearly, how schools are funded going forward has changed. What is unclear is how these changes will be fully implemented and whether the new system will meet the four original goals. Questions linger over whether there will be adequate state funds available to fully implement the changes. The original goal was to add $350 million new dollars annually up to $3.5 billion. However, initial reports from IASA member superintendents indicated that even this amount must be increased to meet the needs for less wealthy school districts.

CORPORATE PERSONAL PROPERTY REPLACEMENT TAX (CPPRT)

Another local source of school district revenue is CPPRT, which was initiated following the abolition of the Illinois Personal Property Tax when the Illinois Constitution was revised in 1970. Unless you are a school business official, you really only need to understand that CPPRT is a state tax on either income or invested capital, on some businesses to replace lost revenue from the abolition of the personal property tax on corporations, partnerships, and other business entities (Illinois Department of Revenue, 2023b).

School districts receive money from state-collected CPPRT taxes each year and treat it as local revenue. Usually, school districts are notified of their estimated CPPRT amount in the summer and receive payments throughout the year. For some school districts, this can be a significant source of revenue. An economic downturn can negatively affect this revenue source. Since school districts have no control over the tax, they merely include CPPRT funds as local revenue in their budget.

SALES TAX REVENUE

Until recently, no school boards were able to generate sales tax revenue. However, a few years ago the legislature passed Public Act 95-675, which allows all counties except Cook to levy a 1% sales tax for school facility purposes through referendum. Revenues received are allocated to schools based on the enrollment of students living in the county (Braun, 2022). Because of the required referendum process, approving a school facilities sales tax in many counties is unfeasible. Most counties, including those in the Chicago area have never even asked voters for approval. However, the following counties have passed the sales tax: Abe Lincoln, Bond, Boone, Brown, Cass, Champaign, Christian, Coles, Cumberland, Douglas, Edgar, Edwards, Egyptian, Fayette, Franklin, Fullerton, Hamilton, Hardin, Henry, Jackson, Jo Daviess, Knox, Laurence, Lee, Livingston, Logan, Macon, Marion, Mason, Macoupin, McDonough, Mercer, Monroe, Montgomery, Peoria, Pike, Randolph, Richland, Rock Island, Saline, Schuyler, Scott, Shelby, Stewardson-Strasburg, Wabash, Warren, Williamson, and Woodford. The tax was rejected by voters in over 20 other counties including Effingham, Hancock, Moultrie, Madison, Sangamon and Union. Many counties have yet to put the referendum before voters. Nonetheless, this revenue option is another source of school funding.

COMPETITIVE GRANTS

Similar to the federal government, state public officials will use specific initiatives to promote their policy agendas. For example, a recent Illinois governor proposed providing all-day kindergarten and reducing primary class size. Rather than distributing funding to all school districts which is not realistic due to limited availability of state funds, he initiated a competitive grant program. Some school districts competed against each other for a fixed pool of dollars.

For some school districts, particularly those with limited revenue, competitive grants, which may include those from private sources, may be an important source of funding. Competitive grants may mean the difference between either offering or not providing much needed programs in cash-strapped school districts.

However, school districts must be careful to ensure that a competitive grant makes educational and financial sense. You may want to ask yourself the following questions when you are considering applying for a competitive grant. How you respond to these will help you decide whether a particular competitive grant is appropriate for your school district.

- Does the purpose of the grant align with district needs?
- Does the grant require the district to provide additional funding?
- How will the faculty and parents react if a grant-funded program is discontinued after two or three years?
- How will the district maintain a grant-based program after funding is discontinued?

FEDERAL AID

Illinois, similar to other states, receives substantial federal education funding. For FY 21, the federal government contributed an estimated $11,236.1 billion or 24.7% percent of general Illinois K-12 public school revenues, which was substantially more than the prior year, primarily due to COVID funding (Illinois State Board of Education, 2022a). These funds are distributed by the federal government to states where they are disbursed primarily as categorical grants to school districts. Examples of the major federal categorical grants include the Federal Lunch Program and Federal Title programs. School districts with larger economically disadvantaged student populations generally receive a higher proportion of need-based federal funding. In addition, the federal government also uses a competitive grant process to promote particular initiatives. The United States Department of Education includes competitive grant information on its website at www.ed.gov. Although federal funding for almost all Illinois school districts is not as substantial a source of school district revenue as are property taxes and state aid, it is none-the-less important for all school districts in this era of limited revenues and rising expenditures.

LOCAL SOURCES

School districts also collect a variety of local user-based fees throughout the school year. Although most of the amounts are relatively small, the revenue is important in times of revenue shortfalls and ever increasing expenditures. Fee increases in financially strapped school districts are often viewed by those without children in school as a preferable option to increase revenues since those who benefit directly are only affected. Local funding sources generally include fees that are established annually by the board of education on the recommendation of the administration.

- School textbook, yearbook, and activity fees (athletic and extracurricular);
- Breakfast and lunch program fees;
- Bus fees;
- Student fines;
- Student technology fees;
- Other program fees such as summer school or after school childcare; and,
- Building rental fees.

INTEREST INCOME

One source of revenue which you may not have considered is investment income. School districts always maintain some reserve funds for cash flow purposes to ensure that they have sufficient dollars available to pay bills and meet their payrolls while waiting for state aid and property tax revenues to arrive. Everyone from individuals to businesses usually have some funds in reserve at any given time.

Laws govern where school districts can invest reserve funds and how they can be used. However, in general, reserves must be kept in low risk, reasonably accessible short-term financial investment vehicles such as certificates of deposit, interest-bearing bank accounts, and government securities, many of which yield interest income (Braun, 2022). School districts with substantial reserves often generate significant interest revenue that can be used to pay operating expenses. In Illinois, investment options are more conservative than in some other states. For districts with large reserves and current operating budget deficits, interest revenue is very important part of the revenue stream.

Although interest income is an important revenue source, a budget deficit can dramatically impact its effectiveness. When a school district is in deficit spending, the dollars needed to make up the deficit come from reserves. As a result, when the school district draws down its reserve to offset a budget deficit, not only does the district have fewer reserves, but also less dollars to invest and therefore reduced income from investments.

ADDITIONAL REVENUE ISSUES

Beyond the sources of revenue already discussed, an understanding of other issues which affect revenues is helpful. Below are several questions and answers, which will clarify other important revenue issues.

- How does the Illinois lottery affect K-12 public school funding?

Almost everyone has heard that the primary argument posed by original lottery proponents was that lottery revenues would benefit public education, right? Well, the truth is that lottery revenues do fund public education and have certainly increased school funding; however, they have not had the impact most citizens expected.

This is a how the process works. Lottery revenues are collected by the state. After paying for prizes and expenses, the profit is placed in the Common School Fund. However, instead of earmarking all lottery funds as new revenue to fund public education, some are used to supplant present funding sources. Political leaders can, if they so choose, say that all lottery dollars went to public education but avoid pointing out that simultaneously other education funding was reduced (Illinois Association of School Boards, 2006a).

- Will school districts continue to receive the level of COVID funding in coming years as they did last school year?

School district should not anticipate receiving Federal Funding related to COVID any longer.

- Why is Illinois allowed to operate with large funding inequities among school districts when other states such as Texas have had their school funding systems declared unconstitutional?

On the surface, this would seem unfair. Yet the reason is quite simple. The Illinois Constitution only states that equitable funding is a goal not a requirement (White, 2007). As a result, no legal basis exists to declare our system unconstitutional. Without a change in the State Constitution, the focus of school funding will likely remain on finding ways to address inequities through the legislative versus judicial process.

- What is a TIF district and how does it affect school district revenues?

A Tax Increment Financing district, TIF, is a tool created through state legislation, which allows municipalities which otherwise would not have adequate resources a vehicle to provide the financial assistance necessary to redevelop blighted areas. In essence, one taxing body, the municipality, is allowed to divert future property tax dollars from another taxing body, a school district, to pay for improvements (Benson, 2006). Common TIF projects include redevelopment of commercial and industrial sites, renovation of existing residential and commercial buildings, acquisition of land, and infrastructure improvements (Illinois Tax Increment Association, 2023).

According to The Illinois Tax Increment Association, under a TIF, the value of the property at the time the TIF is established serves as a baseline. Taxing bodies such as school districts continue to receive property taxes calculated on this "base" or fixed value at the beginning of the TIF for its duration. However, as the property increases in value, the additional taxes generated beyond the "base" are used by the municipality to pay for TIF improvements. The difference between the "base" value of the property and the future increased value is what is referred to as the increment (Illinois Tax Increment Association, 2023).

At the end of the TIF, which is usually 23 years but can be either shorter or longer depending upon need and legal requirements, all taxing bodies ultimately receive the new property value. In almost all instances, the new value is considerably higher since significant improvements were made to the blighted property (Illinois Tax Increment Association, 2023).

School districts are generally negatively affected by a TIF because the value of the property for tax purposes is frozen for many years. Even though ultimately a TIF will likely generate increased property tax revenues, the loss of increases in property tax revenue during the life of the TIF district means less school district revenue.

School administrators working with their boards of education may challenge the validity of a TIF or attempt to negotiate a compromise in the distribution of increased taxes generated during the TIF. At times, this can be an uphill battle. Sometimes this process creates animosity between the two units of government whose interests may be at odds. However, some districts have succeeded in convincing their municipalities to return a portion of TIF funds to their school districts annually. You can increase your chances for some financial consideration if you are cooperative rather than confrontational. It is more effective to work cooperatively with the municipality. At the same time, it is also important to monitor TIF's regularly. Do not assume that your needs will never be considered.

- If you make the assumption that you have two identical homes with all other property tax-related factors held constant across the street from each other, one in Cook County and the other in Lake, why would the Cook homeowner pay less property tax?

Although this scenario as presented is unrealistic, it does demonstrate why Cook County residential taxpayers generally have lower property taxes on properties then those in other counties with similar EAVs. At first look, you might guess that the property taxes are lower because Cook has substantially more business property. However, the actual reason is that Cook County residential properties are assessed by law at 10% while businesses are assessed at a much higher assessment level (25%). This means that businesses pay a larger percentage of taxes than homeowners. Since residential and business property owners in all other counties are assessed at 33%, homeowners theoretically pay the same proportion of property taxes to the school district as businesses.

- What is a tax-exempt school district educational foundation?

In recent years as school districts searched for additional sources of revenue, some have considered establishing educational foundations. In concept, a foundation must be organized as a not-for-profit organization. School district foundations are typically overseen by an independent board that accepts donations and gifts. The foundation board distributes funds as it chooses (Braun, 2022).

Highly successful school district foundations are more the exception than the rule and more prevalent in affluent school districts. Many begin with great enthusiasm but fail due to unsustainable interest and/or lack of substantial funding. These foundations often target specific projects or use funds to encourage innovation. As such, they supplement the current program rather than reduce budget deficits.

There are, though, exceptions. A few Illinois school districts have well-functioning and ongoing foundations, which annually raise substantial revenue. The Stevenson High

School Foundation raised over $600,000 last year, which was used to fund such programs as Kids in Need, Innovation Grants, scholarships and more (Stevenson High School Foundation, 2023).

SUMMARY

In Chapter 3, we have examined the primary sources of school district revenues. Furthermore, we studied the two largest revenue sources: the Illinois property tax and state aid. We also discussed the role politics plays in school governance and funding and additional revenue issues which further impact school district revenues.

Finally, as you have probably surmised, school districts have limited revenue sources. What is equally disconcerting is that school districts have very little influence over the amount of revenue most of these can generate, and for those over which it does have some control such as competitive grants and local fees, the amounts often represent a very small proportion of overall district revenues.

Chapter 4

Expenditures

In Chapter 3, we examined the primary sources of revenue to understand where school districts find the dollars to operate. In this chapter, we will focus our attention on the other side of the equation, expenditures; that is, school district spending. A good starting point for our discussion is to understand the definition of a school district budget as well as the unique accounting structure, fund accounting, under which Illinois public schools function.

SCHOOL DISTRICT BUDGET

What exactly is a school district budget? In its most basic form, a budget is a school district spending plan approved by the local board of education that allows the district administration the authority to spend district funds. Since only the board of education has legal authority to expend district funds, all expenditures must be approved by the board.

FUND ACCOUNTING

In Illinois, school districts are required by law to report school spending through a fund accounting process (Braun, 2022). Fund accounting is very different from that used in the business world and therefore sometimes appears foreign to new school board members and residents.

Under this accounting structure, a school district's budget is divided into several individual funds to which certain revenues are assigned and expenditures deducted. A good way to conceptualize fund accounting is to think of each fund as a separate checkbook established for specific expenses. For example, teacher salaries can be paid from the Education but not the Transportation Fund.

School district budgets are composed of several specific funds which are somewhat expenditure specific and governed by state regulations including transfer restrictions (Braun, 2022). By requiring that certain expenditures be paid from specific funds, Illinois helps ensure that school districts do not, for example, postpone important maintenance projects to fund teachers' salaries. The Illinois State Board of Education defines each of these funds in its 23 Illinois Administrative Code 100.Table A. What is most important for you to understand are not the plethora of requirements associated with fund accounting but rather the structure and basic characteristics of each fund.

BUDGET FUNDS

Education Funds

The Education Fund is by far the largest and most versatile of all funds and is used for the bulk of school district expenditures including educational expenses such as salaries and benefits related to the instructional program, administration, educational materials, staff development, childcare programming, special education, and the lunch program. The Education Fund also includes a sub-fund for Special Education. In fact, any district expense not specifically included in another fund can be paid from the Education Fund.

Operation and Maintenance

Expenses related to the operation and maintenance of facilities including employee salaries, benefits, contractual maintenance, supplies, utilities, and capital improvement projects are included in this fund. Revenues for the Operations and Maintenance Fund come from property taxes, building rental, and interest income.

Transportation

As the name indicates, this fund focuses on transportation expenses. The Transportation Fund receives revenues from property taxes, student fees, and state transportation aid, which are used for such expenditures as driver salaries and benefits, contract bus service costs, gasoline, maintenance, and transportation-related insurances.

Illinois Municipal Retirement and Social Security

Non-certified employees such as teacher assistants or custodians who work a minimum of 600 hours a year participate in a pension plan called the Illinois Municipal Retirement Fund (Illinois Municipal Retirement Fund, 2023). The school board collects property taxes and also utilizes CPPRT and interest to make payments on behalf of eligible employees to IMRF. This fund also pays the board share of social security and Medicare. This fund is supported primarily by property taxes.

Debt Service

The Debt Service Fund (formerly the Bond and Interest Fund) uses tax revenues to pay the principal and interest on bonds and service charges on other long-term debt instruments. Long-term is defined as a minimum of thirteen months. This fund also is used for payment of capital leases for such items as copiers, using funds transferred from the Education Fund.

Capital Projects

This fund is used to pay for major facility related capital improvements. Revenues for this fund can come from property taxes or building bond proceeds.

Fire Prevention and Safety

This fund is limited to paying expenses for capital improvements approved by the State of Illinois as life-safety projects. Revenues for this fund can come from property taxes or life-safety bond proceeds.

Working Cash

For all practical purposes, the Working Cash Fund is a cash flow account that a school district can tap as needs dictate. The Working Cash Fund can accept property tax receipts or proceeds from the sale of certain school bonds; however, no expenditures can be made from it. Rather, this fund can lend dollars as needed to other funds. Some or all of the fund's reserves may be permanently transferred to another fund. Specific laws govern these types of transaction

Tort Immunity and Judgment

The Tort and Immunity and Judgment Fund is used to pay the cost of district insurance and risk management as well as payments for tort judgments. It is funded through tax levies and/or bonds.

EXPENDITURES

Under fund accounting, school district expenditures within each fund are categorized in two ways: purpose and type. First, expenditures are designated by their purpose or "function":

- Instruction
- Support Services
- Community Services
- Debt Service
- Payment to Other Districts and Governmental Units

Within each of the above categories, expenditures are further assigned to a specific subcategory. For example, in the Education Fund, instruction expenditures are defined as one of ten sub-purposes:

- Regular Programs
- Special Education Programs
- Adult/Continuing Education
- Vocational Programs
- Interscholastic Programs
- Summer School Programs
- Gifted Programs
- Bilingual Programs
- Truant Alternative & Optional Programs

In addition to being categorized by purpose, Expenditures must also be identified by type or "object." As a result, each is assigned to one of the following:

- Salaries
- Employee Benefits
- Purchased Services
- Supplies & Materials
- Capital Outlay
- Other Objects
- Non-Capitalized Equipment
- Termination Benefits

To illustrate this process, let's consider how the cost of board-paid teacher dental insurance would be designated. First, it would be charged to the Education Fund since it is an educational expense. It would be further categorized under Instruction as Regular Programs and an Employee Benefit.

This accounting code system was created to achieve some comparability and accountability in reporting among Illinois school districts. Under this system, the Illinois State Board of Education is able to generate a variety of reports of which the most recognizable is the Illinois State School Report Card, an accountability document aimed at the public.

Definitions of Type-Categories

Although some of the sub-categories such as salaries and employee benefits are self-explanatory, the others require some definition. Please find below examples of the most common categories of expenditures found under these.

Purchased Services

- Consultants
- Legal fees
- Copier maintenance
- Contract services such as the lunch program
- Building services such as heating, ventilation, and air conditioning maintenance

Supplies and Materials

- Instructional materials
- Office supplies, cleaning products
- Utility costs
- Food products

Capital Outlay (Durable items usually over $2000 designed to be used for multiple years)

- Computers
- Busses
- Construction projects

Other Objects

- Membership dues
- Bond payments
- Tuition for special education students
- Transfers

Non-Capitalized Equipment

- Durable items between $500 - $2000

Termination Benefits

- Payments to terminated or retiring employees as compensation for unused sick and vacation days

Chapter 4

BUDGET REQUIREMENTS

Annual Financial Reports

Besides ensuring continuity of school district financial reporting, the prescribed fund accounting procedures are essential to the completion of various state reports. Discussed below are several reports which must either be completed by the school district or generated by the Illinois State Board of Education based on school-district supplied data. School districts are required to submit their budgets after local school board approval to the ISBE by the end of September. Since it is a budget, this is the school district spending plan for the year.

After the end of the fiscal year, school districts submit a report entitled the Annual Financial Report (AFR), which documents the actual spending of district funds. The district's revenues and expenditures are verified as part of the mandated annual audit conducted by an independent outside municipal accounting firm. Both of these are prepared under the ISBE-mandated fund accounting structure.

Annual School District Audit

School districts are required to have their financial records audited annually by an independent auditor approved the board of education. The primary purpose of an audit is to examine the school district's financial records to determine if they fairly represent the school district's financial position. The audit also provides a review of the school district's internal bookkeeping procedures and controls.

Deficit Reduction Plan

School districts that operate under an overall deficit budget must complete a mandated Deficit Reduction Plan in which they explain how they plan to eliminate their deficit (Braun, 2022). This process emerged after a school district reached a severe financial crisis stage and the state legislature determined that the school district financial monitoring process was not adequate. For this report, the definition of deficit is different from that used in our earlier discussion of an annual district deficit.

When we discussed local school district deficits in Chapter 1, a budget deficit was defined as any yearly budget in which expenditures exceeded revenues. Districts, though, even with annual budget deficits, usually have sufficient reserves to offset anticipated shortfalls. Under the Deficit Reduction Plan, these districts would not be required to submit a plan. Only those school districts which did not have projected reserves to offset the projected deficit must develop a budget reduction plan. Since most districts, even those with annual budget deficits generally have some reserves, only those in the most financial difficulty would be required to do so.

Administrative Cost Cap

Since FY99, school districts have been required to limit administrative expenditure increases to 5%. School district administrators must ensure that designated budget line items related to administrative costs do not exceed this limit when submitting their school district's annual budget and Annual Financial Report to ISBE (Braun, 2022).

Fiduciary Responsibility

School district employees and school board members have an important ethical and moral obligation to manage and account for school district funds, especially for the benefit of students. This is called their fiduciary responsibility.

SCHOOL DISTRICT FINANCIAL PROFILE

Annually, all Illinois school districts receive a School District Rating from the Illinois State Board of Education. Its primary purpose is to analyze and monitor the finances of school districts (Illinois State Board of Education, 2023e).

The Illinois State Board of Education utilizes five financial indicators in arriving at a district's designation.

- Fund balance to revenue ratio
- Expenditure to revenue ratio
- Days cash on hand
- Percent of short-term borrowing ability remaining
- Percentage of long-term debt margin remaining

Using a quantitative score and weighting system for the indicator, school districts are assigned to one of four categories:

- Financial Recognition
- Financial Review
- Financial Early Warning
- Financial Watch

For most school districts, the School District Financial Profile has relatively little significance. Its greatest impact is primarily political. For example, it is not uncommon for a school district to be rated in the Financial Recognition category because at the moment it has an overall reserve but at the same time is trending toward financial difficulty due to a growing school budget deficit. The high rating may be a stumbling block for school districts that hope to pass an operating fund referendum now rather than wait until the district is approaching a crisis. More specific information on the Illinois

School District Financial Profile system is available on the Illinois State Board of Education website (http://www.isbe.net) under School Finance.

BUDGETING METHODS

School districts use various methods to establish the actual budget amount in line items particularly at the school level. Costs for such items as salaries and benefits are generally linked to staffing levels, negotiated contracts, insurance premiums, and local board policies and therefore are calculated based on these factors. However, for school-level budget items for which the administration has substantial control such as instructional materials, supplies, and capital expenditures, district level administrators often approach the budgeting process from different perspectives. The two most common budget allocations approaches are fixed allocation and zero-based budgeting.

Fixed Allocation

A popular approach employed by school district central office administrators to allocate funds for district programs and individual schools is the fixed allocation method. Through this approach, usually a fixed percentage often tied to the rate of inflation is allocated to each district program area and individual schools. For example, a building principal may receive a set percentage increase for all grade levels and subject areas for instructional materials and supplies. Through this method, each grade level, subject area, or other building-level program receives a fixed percentage increase.

However, it is common under this approach for the superintendent to allow principals the discretion to adjust the distribution of the overall allocation between line items as deemed necessary. However, the overall amount allocated to the school is fixed at a certain percentage or dollar amount. Also, in instances where enrollment fluctuations occur, special programs are implemented, or unique capital needs exist, additional dollars may be allocated beyond the fixed amount.

Zero-Based Budgeting

This approach to budget allocation, which emerged in the 1970s, was called zero-based budgeting. Although it is less prevalent today, nonetheless, some school districts use this approach or some variance of it to set allocation levels. The concept behind the zero-based budgeting model is that funds should only be allocated based on actual needs, and thereby reduce unnecessary spending. Under zero-based budgeting, funds are allocated based on projected needs rather than prior year's funding levels. For example, school principals would be required to "make a case" for all budget fund requests. Through this process, they would need to justify program needs before actual budgeted amounts would be established.

It is, though, often criticized as too time consuming or unnecessary since allocations are often too small to justify the additional work entailed to implement. The use of a full zero-based budget model is not common; however, it is not usual for school districts to employ elements of the model as part of a fixed allocation process.

STUDENT ACTIVITY FUND

In addition to the regular budget accounts, school districts maintain student activity accounts as well as convenience or fiduciary funds. Student activity accounts are typically used to manage funds from student-related clubs and activities. These are under the direction of the school board, superintendent, or district employees. Fiduciary funds are maintained by the district as convenience accounts. Examples include funds from parent, employee, and other non-student groups A common example is a school's Social Fund. Teachers collect dollars from staff members, which are used to purchase gifts for events such as births, weddings, illness, and retirements (Braun, 2022).

Although these accounts are separate from those of the district, school boards have a fiduciary responsibility under the Illinois School Code, Section 10-20.19(3), to manage all funds properly even though activity fund accounts are not district funds. As such, school boards must establish policies and administrative procedures to meet their fiduciary responsibility. Different management requirements apply to the two types of funds. It is important to note that activity funds are audited during the annual school district audit (Braun, 2022).

Even though school boards have the legal responsibility for activity fund accounts, day-to-day management typically rests with the administration. As a result, administrators must be especially vigilant managing all aspects of the activity fund process. This is especially important since activity fund revenues are often cash-based and handled by parents, teachers, and support personnel (Braun, 2022).

SUMMARY

The focus of this chapter was the expenditure side of the equation. After discussing what constitutes a school district budget, we examined Illinois fund accounting requirements. We also studied budget requirements, the state School District Financial Profile system, and common approaches school districts employ to determine program and building-level budget allocations.

Chapter 5

Tax Caps

One of the most often misunderstood pieces of Illinois school finance legislation is the Property Tax Extension Limitation Law (PTELL) or as it is usually called – the property tax cap, which was created to slow the escalating growth of property taxes.

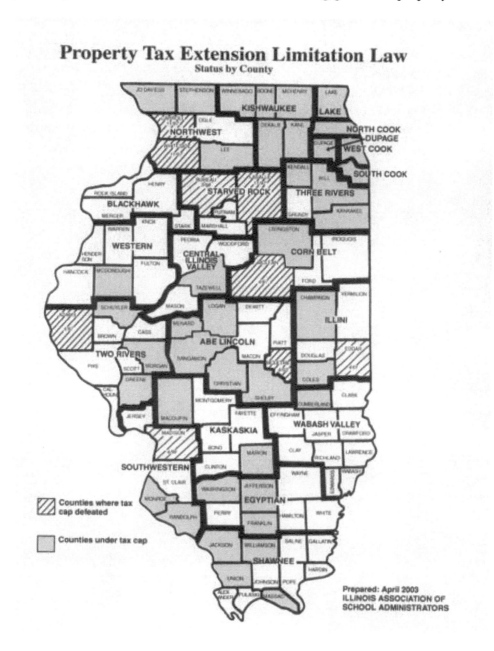

Property Tax Extension Limitation Law
Status by County

Prepared: April 2003
ILLINOIS ASSOCIATION OF
SCHOOL ADMINISTRATORS

PTELL initially included only the collar counties of Chicago (DuPage, Kane, Lake, McHenry, and Will) when it was passed in 1991 was subsequently extended to Cook in 1994. Ultimately, all Illinois counties were given the option to extend PTELL to property in their counties although not all chose to do so. (Illinois Department of Revenue, 2023a). The figure above shows the latest status of the tax cap in Illinois counties (Illinois Department of Revenue, 2023a).

TAX CAP PROVISIONS

In order to slow the growth of property taxes, legislators focused the tax cap on the governmental units' property tax extensions, the amount of property taxes the school district received the prior year. Therefore, under PTELL, a school district's property tax extension can increase annually up to 5% or the rate of inflation as measured by the All- Urban Consumer Price Index (CPI), whichever is less. Since 1990, the CPI has not exceeded 5% until this year. The history of the PTELL limit for most years (Illinois Department of Revenue, 2023a) is shown in the table below.

Table 5.1
History of CPI

Year	December CPI-U	% CPI Increase from Prior Year	% PTELL Limit	Levy Year	Year Taxes Paid
1993	145.8	2.7	2.7 (5% for Cook)	1994	1995
1994	149.7	2.7	2.7	1995	1996
1998	163.9	1.6	1.6	1999	2000
2000	174.0	3.4	3.4	2001	2002
2001	176.7	1.6	1.6	2002	2003
2002	180.9	2.4	2.4	2003	2004
2003	184.3	1.9	1.9	2004	2005
2004	190.3	3.3	3.3	2005	2006
2005	196.8	3.4	3.4	2006	2007
2006	201.8	2.5	2.5	2007	2008
2007	210.036	4.08	4.1	2008	2009
2008	210.228	0.1	0.1	2009	2010
2009	215.949	2.7	2.7	2010	2011
2010	219.179	1.5	1.5	2011	2012
2011	225.672	3.0	3.0	2012	2013
2012	229.601	1.7	1.7	2013	2014
2013	233.049	1.5	1.5	2014	2015
2014	234.812	0.8	0.8	2015	2016
2015	236.525	0.7	0.7	2016	2017
2016	241.432	2.1	2.1	2017	2018
2017	246.524	2.1	2.1	2018	2019
2018	251.233	1.9	1.9	2019	2020
2019	256.974	2.3	2.3	2020	2021
2020	260.474	1.4	1.4	2021	2022
2021	278.802	7.0	5.0%	2022	2023
2022	296.797	6.5	5.0%	2023	2024

To illustrate how the tax cap works, let's consider an example. If a school district has a property tax extension of $20,000,000 in tax year 2022 and the tax cap for the 2023 levy is 5.0%, the 2023 extension is limited to 5.0% more than the 2022 extension or $21,000,000 in taxes on existing property, which will be collected in calendar year 2024.

Limiting property tax revenues to the CPI or 5% can be especially onerous to growing school districts. Therefore, when PTELL became law, a provision was included which allows school districts to receive increased property taxes beyond the 5% or CPI level for something called "new growth."

Without some provision for additional revenues with increasing enrollment, this could be a real problem for school districts. For example, what would a school district do if it experienced a substantial increase in enrollment because of a new townhouse development but could only increase its property tax revenue by 1.4%? Fortunately, legislators recognized this issue when they designed PTELL.

NEW GROWTH PROVISION

Since communities are constantly evolving, legislators recognized that some provision was needed to adjust for changes such as enrollment growth. The provision, commonly referred to as "new growth," allows school districts to levy additional property taxes for increases in the assessed value related to new construction and other improvements (Illinois Department of Revenue, 2023c).

Consider this typical example. Your school district has a large parcel of vacant land. A developer receives approval to build a subdivision, which increases the enrollment of the local school district by 200 students. If it costs $12,000 to educate each student, where would you find $2,400,000 to pay for these children's education, particularly if your property tax extension was limited to 1.4%?

Under the new growth provision of PTELL, the school district can capture the additional property tax revenue generated by the new property, which is exempt from the tax cap for the first year. This means that new property including residences and business property such as office buildings, shopping centers, and industrial facilities will generate additional property tax revenues beyond the cap (Kersten, 2008). The property taxes resulting from new growth may or may not be sufficient to pay the costs incurred for the additional children in this instance, but are nonetheless important. However, the school district must levy for it the first year it comes onto the tax roles or permanently lose taxes that otherwise would be attributable to the new growth.

CALCULATING NEW GROWTH

To illustrate how the new growth provision increases revenues, let's consider an example below. For illustration purposes, we will assume that the school district had a property tax extension for tax year 2022 of $20,000,000. The CPI (tax cap rate) for the next year is 5.0%. As we discussed earlier, under PTELL, the school district can receive $21,000,000 in property taxes for the coming year (an increase of 5.0% over the prior year), even if actual property values increased more than 5.0%.

However, during the year, a new hotel was placed on the tax rolls. After completing the tax assessment process, the tax extension office calculated that hotel would generate another $200,000 in additional property taxes based on the district's tax rate. Because of the new growth provision, the school district was eligible to receive both the $21,000,000 plus the additional $200,000. As a result, the new extension base for the following year would be $21,200,000. As you can see, this provision is very important to tax capped school districts especially in property poor school districts, which most need every possible tax dollar available.

Table 5.2
Extension with New Growth

2020 Tax Extension	$20,000,000
2020 CPI (1.4%)	X 5.0
Maximum Collectable Taxes	$21,000,000
Hotel Property Tax Revenue	+ 200,000
New Extension Base	$21.200,000

HOME IMPROVEMENT EXEMPTION

Not all new growth is immediately available to taxing bodies. Under Illinois law, the first $25,000 of EAV on new residential property is tax deferred for four years (Illinois Department of Revenue, 2023c). After the fourth year, though, the $25,000 is included in the new growth figure for the following year. If a residential improvement exceeds the $25,000 figure, the amount over the exclusion is treated as new growth immediately (Kersten, 2008).

What is especially important to understand is that school districts make their property tax levy requests in December, months before assessments are finalized and the new growth figure is calculated. Since school districts do not know the amount of new growth, they must make their best guess on what amount to levy the prior December. As a result, school administrators often advise school boards to "balloon" levy, that is, ask for more property taxes than they think they are likely to receive, so that when the property tax extension is ultimately finalized, the district receives every property tax dollar permitted under PTELL, including the amount that results from new growth.

COMMON MISCONCEPTION

The most frequent misconception about the tax cap is that it caps individual property owners' tax bills. It does not. What it actually does is slow their rate of growth. PTELL caps the district's property tax extension (amount of property taxes the school districts is entitled to receive), which actually caps the revenue growth.

To understand this difference, let's consider how an individual's residential property tax is determined (See table below). The process begins with the county tax extension office calculating the total amount of Equalized Assessed Valuation (EAV) within the boundaries of the school district. For our sample school district, the total EAV is $500,000,000. In our scenario, the individual homeowner has an EAV of $50,000. This means that the homeowner's EAV is 0.0001% of the total district EAV. Therefore, the individual property owners would pay 0.0001% of the amount of property taxes due the school district. If the school district's property tax extension was $20,000,000, the homeowner would receive a bill for $2,000 or 0.0001 of $20,000,000.

Table 5.3
Proportion of EAV Calculation

Total District EAV	$500,000,000
Homeowner's EAV	$50,000
Homeowner's EAV Portion of Total EAV	0.0001
Total School District Property Tax Revenue	$20,000,000
Homeowner's Property Tax Bill	$2,000
Tax Calculation	$20,000,000 X 0.0001 = $2,000

However, some property owners could actually pay higher taxes if their proportion of the overall EAV goes up faster than someone else's (See table below). For example, if you added a home addition or made some other improvement, which increased your EAV, you would own a higher proportion of the overall EAV. Therefore, when the county extension office calculates your property tax bill, because your portion of the overall EAV is larger due to the building addition, you would pay more property taxes.

In our example, if we assume that the overall EAV remained at $500,000,000 and the homeowner's EAV increased to $65,000, the individual now has a higher percent of overall EAV (0.00013) and will pay a higher percentage of the overall property tax requested by the school district or $2,600.

Table 5.4
Proportion of EAV with Homeowner Addition

Total School District EAV	$500,000,000
Homeowner's EAV	$65,000
Homeowner's EAV Portion of Total EAV	0.00013
Total School District Property Tax Revenue	$20,000,000
Homeowner's Property Tax Bill	$2,600
Tax Calculation	$20,000,000 X 0.00013 = $2,600

Homeowners could also see their property tax bills increase due to a decrease in the overall EAV. The most common reasons that the overall EAV would decrease are either a reduction of EAV due to a business property tax appeal or a decrease in the multiplier. In Cook County where, unlike other counties, the multiplier is more than 1.0 traditionally and tends to vary from year to year.

If the overall EAV goes down but a homeowner's EAV remains the same, the property owner has a higher percentage of the overall EAV. The table below provides an example of this scenario.

Table 5.5
Effect of lower Overall EAV

Total School District EAV	$480,000,000
Homeowner's EAV	$50,000
Homeowner's EAV Portion of Total EAV	0.0001041
Total District Property Tax Revenue	$20,000,000
Homeowner's Property Tax Bill	$2,083
Tax Calculation	$20,000,000 X 0.0001041 = $2,083

The opposite is also true. If, for example, the county re-assesses all property in the area and raises other property owners' assessments faster than yours, you now have a smaller proportion of the overall EAV and may be taxed less.

Although the actual property tax increase or decrease in this instance would be small, it does demonstrate how the concept of ownership of a proportion of EAV affects an individual's property tax bill.

TAX CAP REFERENDUM OPTIONS

Since the passage of PTELL, tax capped school districts are limited to specific options when requesting an operating rate increase. These are discussed in more detail in Chapter 9.

BUSINESS PROPERTY TAX APPEALS

Other factors can also affect a taxpayer's proportion of overall property taxes. The most significant are business property tax appeals. You have probably heard that large businesses regularly appeal their property tax assessments. Many negotiate lower assessment levels through the county assessor or take their case to the Board of Review before the extension is set. Property owners who choose to challenge their assessments may further appeal to the county Property Tax Appeals Board (PTAB) or the circuit court (Illinois Department of Revenue, 2023c). Some, of course, study their assessments and realize that they are not likely to win a reduction.

What the public does not understand is that under the tax cap, when a business receives a tax assessment reduction, this translates into a tax increase for other taxpayers, including many residential property owners. This is because a reduction in a business' property assessment means that the business now owns a smaller proportion of the overall EAV. Other property owners now have higher proportions of the overall EAV and must pay a greater percentage of property taxes.

EFFECT OF TAX CAP

From any school district's perspective, the property tax cap law is detrimental because it substantially limits school district revenues. Other sources of revenue such as state aid do not offset the limiting effects of PTELL. The reality is that school districts must operate with their major source of revenue, property taxes, artificially capped while their costs often increase faster than the rate of inflation and are uncapped.

Consider the following questions to appreciate this point.

- How much have healthcare costs increased annually?
- Have your utility costs risen faster than inflation?
- How much have college tuition risen in recent years?
- Have teacher salaries increased more than the rate of inflation?

These questions illustrate how difficult it is to manage a school district under the tax cap, particularly if you hope to maintain current levels of programs and services, when revenues are restricted and expenditures are not. This is probably the most significant factor contributing to school district deficit spending and financial stress in Illinois.

During a few recent years, though, the tax cap has actually proven helpful. Under provision of the cap, only the school district tax extension is actually capped. This means that when property assessments decline, school districts are still entitled to the amount of revenue allowed under the law. Therefore, taxpayers are required to pay for all property taxes the school district is entitled to receive even though their property assessments have declined. What occurs is that the county merely raises the district's tax rate to accommodate the adjustment. With property values now on the increase, this quirk in the law is likely to become less relevant.

TAX CAP AND POLITICS

When was the last time you heard an Illinois politician say, "Let's raise property taxes" or "Let's eliminate PTELL" when presenting their campaign platform? We all know that it is popular to be anti-tax. As educational stakeholders, we understand the realities of school funding and cannot understand why our political leaders do not. We need to recognize that one of a politician's goals is re-election. With this goal in mind, politicians tend to be particularly sensitive to all aspects of the political process, especially constituent views. As a result, it is wise to anticipate that politicians will typically act in a political manner. If taxpayers believe that property taxes are too high and that the tax cap is a plus, you can be assured that the cap will not be repealed.

Similarly, at the district level, a substantial percentage of local residents have no direct vested interest in schools. Some never had or no longer have children in schools while others are on fixed or low incomes. These groups have little incentive to increase property taxes. School board members and administrators must recognize these realities and be prepared to respond whether at school budget and tax levy hearings or during school board elections and school referendum campaigns.

MONITORING LEGISLATION

In recent years, Illinois legislators have proposed limiting the cost of living (Consumer Price Index - CPI) increases provided under PTELL for school districts that have overall EAV decreases from the prior year. Most recently, the legislature considered freezing property tax rates statewide in relation to changing from a fixed to graduated state income tax model. At present, the property tax rate freeze is on hold, while a governor appointed task force studies Illinois property taxes in general. You can be assured that such issues will continue to receive political consideration. As a result, it is imperative that educational stakeholders be vigilant legislative observers.

SUMMARY

In Chapter 5, we have explored the legal requirements of the Illinois Property Tax Extension Limitation Law in order to understand how the tax cap impacts public school funding at the district level. In particular, we examined how it limits school district property tax revenues and learned that its main purpose is to slow the rate property owners' tax increases rather than set an actual cap on an individual's property tax. We also considered the impact of PTELL's new growth provision as well as political issues which all educational stakeholders must consider in the tax cap era.

School administrators, school board members, and other public education proponents, should closely monitor all legislative initiatives. Because school funding is at the forefront of everyone's political agendas, those with a vested interest in public education must become informed advocates for schools. They must help legislators understand the pragmatic implications of any potential legislation.

Chapter 6

Borrowing

This chapter will focus on additional options to fund school district operations: short and long-term borrowing and capital leasing. Part of the long-term borrowing discussion will explore the impact of the property tax cap law (PTELL) on the ability of school districts to issue bonds.

SHORT-TERM BORROWING

The most widely used form of short-term borrowing is the tax anticipation warrant (TAW). They are analogous to personal payday loans which individuals receive and must pay back from their next paychecks. As the name implies, a school board borrows money from a financial institution and agrees to pay back the loan with interest from taxes it anticipates receiving in the near future. In fact, by law TAWs must be paid back on a set date after the property tax receipts arrive. A school board may borrow up to 85% of the property taxes it has levied in the fund for which the warrant is issued and repaid when taxes are received (Braun, 2022).

The primary purpose of TAWs is for cash flow needs. Typically, a school district will sell tax anticipation warrants when it does not have sufficient funds available in its reserves to make payments due to employees or vendors. To some degree, TAWs are similar to credit card debt. If, for example, you need to repair your car and do not have money on hand but will soon, you may charge the repair on your credit card and pay it when the bill comes due.

Yet, similar to a person who has very little savings and has difficulty meeting unexpected expenditures, school districts that use TAWs tend to be the poorer districts with larger budget deficits and small reserves. TAWs also are an indication of financial weakness.

To illustrate this further, let's consider an example of events which forced some school districts to sell TAWs. In 2021/2022, the Cook County Assessor continued the complex task of modernizing its technological framework, a plan that had been in place since 2015, but coordination with the Cook County Board of Review became problematic. The result was a five month delay in property tax bills causing cash flow shortages for many schools districts in Fall of 2022. The delay is expected to occur again in Fall of 2023. As the political wrangling continued, school districts were forced to dip into their reserves to pay salaries and other costs. For those school districts that had reserves, the primary negative effects were the loss of interest or having to sell a security early at a loss due to the property taxes received late. For the least wealthy districts, they not only lost interest revenue but also had to borrow money through tax anticipation warrants then pay interest on the loans too! Again, the poorest districts were impacted the most.

In addition to TAWs, you should be aware that several other short-term borrowing options exist that employed less regularly than TAWs. Unless you are in business management, you do not need to understand the specific differences. However, you should at least recognize that other options are available. If you find yourself in a situation where additional financial counsel is needed, you would most likely seek advance from specialists. Other short-term options include:

- Tax anticipation notes;
- General obligation tax anticipation warrants;
- Corporate personal property replacement tax notes;
- Revenue anticipation notes; and,
- Teachers' orders.

LONG-TERM BORROWING

Another potential source of revenues which school boards may to want consider is classified as long-term borrowing. Several distinct borrowing types are available to many school districts, each with its own unique requirements. However, before examining each of these individually, it is important to understand both the concept and legal requirements of school district debt service extension base (Illinois Department of Revenue, 2022e). The extension is the amount of property taxes received the prior year.

Debt Service Extension Base

In Illinois school finance and politics, sometimes it is better to be lucky than good. So is the case with the debt extension limit. When the tax cap became law, a provision was included which established a permanent debt extension limit for school districts. The debt service extension base, which represented the existing school district debt, was based on the actual dollar amount of the tax extension in a school district's Debt Service Fund the year following passage of PTELL (Illinois Department of Revenue, 2023e).

As you can imagine, the amount of the limit was extremely variable since it was not tied to the financial position of the district or any logical factors such as need, but merely the tax extension amount at a particular point in time. Those districts which happen to be lucky enough to have a large extension were winners while those which had no Debt Service levy that year were losers.

Let's examine how the debt service extension base actually works. If your school district was fortunate enough to have outstanding non-referendum bonds with a repayment in 1994 of $2,000,000, you now have a permanent $2M debt service extension base. This means that you can tax property owners up to $2M each year to pay the principal and interest on outstanding bonds. In other words, the school district may sell bonds whose payment schedule equals $2M each year including principal and interest.

What makes this a source of additional revenue is that you are able to tax the public in addition to the tax cap amount. If you were unfortunate and had no existing debt, you have two referendum options. First, you can ask the public for approval to sell bonds. Second, you can go to referendum to establish a specific debt extension service base.

Beginning with the 2009 tax levy, school districts' debt service extension bases increased annually by the lesser of 5% or the CPI from the prior calendar year. This provision is important because school boards have the potential to generate additional revenues due to the increases in the amount of bonds they are permitted to repay. Since they can tax the property owners more, they can also increase the amount they borrow.

Bonds

What exactly is a bond? In its most basic form, a bond is a loan often in $5,000 amounts that the school district makes and agrees to pay back over some specified period of time much as you might an automobile loan. Bonds must be issued for a specific purpose. School boards, which meet specific legal requirements, have the authority to issue certain types of bonds.

For the purpose of illustration, we will assume that a school board has authority to sell $7,500,000 in bonds, which will be repaid over four years without referendum but subject to the $2M debt extension limitation in the example. As such, the district will sell the bonds, generally to large financial institutions that either include them in investment portfolios or re-sell them to other investors. As a result of the sale, the school district receives $7.5M. If issued as tax exempt bonds (lower interest rate), the 7.5M must be used for capital projects and spent in three years. If issued as taxable bonds, the the $7.5M may be placed in the school district's reserves and used as needed.

The bond holders are repaid their $7.5M plus interest over the term of the bonds i.e. the next three years. To make these re-payments, the school district is allowed to add the repayment cost to its Debt Service Fund levy annually but cannot receive revenue beyond the debt extension limit of $2M.

Bond Sale Process

What are the basic steps a school district takes to complete a Working Cash or Funding Bond sale? Although these can vary somewhat, Elizabeth Hennessy (Hennessy, 2019), bond consultant for Raymond James & Associates, explains that a regular bond sale process normally includes:

- Discussing with the school board a financial plan, approval by the Board of a Resolution of Intent to sell bonds, and scheduling a public hearing (School District);
- Publishing the notices of intent and of public in a local paper (Bond Consultant);
- Preparing preliminary bond sale documents (Bond Consultant);
- Holding a meeting with bond rating company to establish the district's bond rating (School District, Rating Agency, and Bond Consultant);
- Conducting a public hearing at a regular school board meeting (School Board);

- Approving the Bond resolution and conducting the bond sale (Bond Consultant, School District, and Attorney); and,
- Closing the sale of bonds (School District, Bond Consultant, & Bond Attorney)

You will note from the steps above that school administrators need to understand the general process but not be experts. Rather, they employ outside consultants and legal experts to facilitate their bond sales.

TYPES OF BONDS

Now that we have discussed the debt extension limit, defined bonds, and examined the basic bond sale process, we are ready to consider five of the most common types of school district bonds: Working Cash, Life-safety, Funding, Alternate Bonds, Debt Certificates, and Building Bonds.

Working Cash Bonds

A prominent type of bond is the Working Cash Bond. Proceeds from a Working Cash Bond sale are deposited in the Working Cash Fund. From there, they can be loaned or transferred as needed to other operating funds for use for capital projects or operations (Braun, 2022). If bond proceeds are loaned, they must be paid back to the Working Cash Fund when tax dollars are received.

Let's consider some examples.

- If a school district sells $7.5M in Working Cash Bonds while operating under a $1M deficit in the Education Fund, it can transfer $1M from Working Cash to cover the deficit.
- School districts may use bond proceeds for facility renovation. If, for instance, a school district needs $2M to fund a school renovation project but only has $1M available in its Operations and Maintenance Fund, it has the option to transfer the $1M needed from the Working Cash Fund.

Working Cash Fund Bond Requirements

School districts are subject to certain requirements when they initiate a Working Cash Bond sale. First, if they want to sell the bonds as federal tax free, they must show that the funds are needed to operate the district in the immediate future. If not, the district is free to sell them as taxable bonds. Some investors are particularly interested in tax free bonds and are willing to buy them at a lower interest rate, which means that the school district will pay less interest on the bonds (Braun, 2022).

Another important fact is that Working Cash Bonds are subject to a "backdoor referendum." The term makes the sale sound "sneaky" but it is not. School districts which meet legal requirements to sell these bonds must pass a motion at an open school board meeting and publish a notice of intent to sell bonds in a local newspaper 30 days before any action. The school board then must hold a public hearing before the actual bond sale. During this time period, residents may force the school board to take the bond sale to a referendum if they can obtain the signatures of 10% of the registered voters on a petition which is submitted to the school board. The school board at this point may either hold a referendum or drop the sale. Absent the petition, the Board may proceed with the sale.

Life-Safety Bonds

Back in 1958, a horrible event occurred in the Chicago-area, which led to the creation of the Life-Safety Code. This was the Our Lady of Angels fire which resulted in the deaths of many adults and children (Our Lady of Angels Fire Memorial, 2008). This event gave impetus to the State of Illinois Life-Safety Code which contains facility standards for public schools.

Every ten years, school districts are required to hire an architect who completes a life-safety audit of school district facilities. In this report, the architect identifies any areas which fail to meet life-safety requirements and therefore may qualify for funding either through life-safety bonds or the district's life-safety levy. The architect must prepare special documents called Life-Safety Amendments which are submitted to the Illinois State Board of Education that makes the final determination on whether the project qualifies for life-safety (Braun, 2022).

For larger ISBE-approved amendments, school districts with debt service extension bases may find that the bond sale approach is preferred. For example, a common Life-Safety improvement is the replacement of a school roof. Rather, than use funds from the Operations and Maintenance Fund, a school district with a debt service extension base may sell Life-Safety Bonds to pay for the repair.

Life-Safety Fund Requirements

The most significant difference between Life-Safety and Working Cash Bonds is that the district is not subject to the backdoor referendum process for the Life-Safety bonds. In fact, the school board can sell the bonds simply by taking action at an open school board meeting following a public hearing (Braun, 2022). However, remember that a district in a tax capped county without a debt extension limit cannot realistically use this bond sale option because they would have to repay the bonds from regular revenues creating a shortage of funds in other budgeted areas. Also, school districts must plan well in advance of any planned Life-Safety bond sale since approval by both the Regional Office of Education and the state can make the process quite time consuming.

Debt Certificates

School boards may issue debt certificates for capital projects. Debt certificates are paid from the general funds of the District. There is no separate bond or interest tax levy dedicated to the repayment of debt certificates. The District annually budgets a sufficient amount to pay the principal and interest on debt certificates. These certificates are repaid from to the debt service extension base but operating fund revenue sources such as O&M tax levy, corporate and personal property replacement taxes, evidence based funding from the state and other non-restricted revenues.

Debt certificates offer the advantage of spreading capital costs over several budget years. They also help preserve fund balances and may be a preferred alternative when interest rates are low. On the other hand, they are not an additional revenue source but do require the school district to pay interest (Hennessy, 2023).

Funding Bonds

Funding bonds, which are subject to the debt extension limit in tax capped counties, can be sold to pay for incurred district obligations (bills). Two common uses of these bonds include paying for computer hardware or buses already purchased by the school district. However, since they are subject to a backdoor referendum, you should be caution using them. If the taxpayer challenge is successful and the district does not pass a referendum, the district must still pay for these capital items. If you are considering funding bonds, it is advisable to consult a bond attorney to ensure you understand all bond sale requirements and any potential implications.

Non-Taxed Capped Counties

School districts in non-tax capped counties have a distinct advantage over those subject to PTELL. Since they are not subject to the tax cap, they generally can sell both Working Cash and Life-Safety Bonds because their debt repayment is not limited by the debt service extension base (Illinois Department of Revenue, 2022e). The primary concern for these school districts is convincing their school boards to proceed with the bond sale and ensuring that any increase associated with the bond repayment does not create consternation among local taxpayers.

Alternate Bonds and the One Percent County School Facility Cent Sales Tax

In counties where voters have approved through referendum a one per cent sales tax for county school facilities, the school board may issue bonds to pay for improvements. Bond maturities may not exceed 40 years. These bonds are not subject to the debt service extension base or a backdoor referendum. However, a separate fund must be established to account for revenues and expenses. Alternate bonds also have a bond and interest tax levy associated with them that must be abated annually as the sales tax or other pledged revenue is received. School districts may also issue alternate bonds for school corporate purposes, budgeting an operating fund revenue source, similar to debt certificates. These alternate bonds are subject to backdoor referendum and public hearing.

Building Bonds

The final category of long-term borrowing we will consider is Building Bonds. These are the types of bonds with which you may be familiar because they require a referendum. When a school board wants to fund the construction of a major project such as a building addition or new school, it will often proceed with a referendum because it does not have sufficient reserves to fund the project.

A school board may hold a referendum during any general election except during fall elections during odd years. If the bond sale is approved by a majority of the voters, the district may proceed. Bond proceeds are used to complete the project and additional taxes are levied over a specified period of time to pay back the bond holders with interest. These bonds are not limited by the debt service extension base (Braun, 2022).

These bonds that are, in essence, tied to "brick and mortar" are typically paid back over many years. Unlike Working Cash Bonds, which often fund operational costs, Building Bonds improve facilities for generations of students, some of whom may not yet be born. Consequently, it is common to extend debt repayment over many years to ensure that those who will benefit form the improvements share in the costs.

Other Available Bond Options

Although we examined the three most prevalent types of bonds: Working Cash, Life-Safety, and Building, other variations of bonds and short-term borrowing are available. According to Braun, (2022) two others rarely used available include:

- Tort judgment; and,
- Insurance reserve.

For all but school business officials, an extended discussion of these is unnecessary. Most school district administrators and school boards considering a bond sale will need to seek advice from bond consultants to identify and understand their options.

Intergovernmental Borrowing

A relatively recent borrowing option available to school districts is loaning money to other school districts. This option is especially effective for funding short-term debt such as Tax Anticipation Warrants (TWAs). It can also be a win/win for both school districts. School districts with excess reserves can earn higher rates of return by lending funds to needy school districts. In return, those borrowing money can save on borrowing costs (Hennessy, Connor, & Prombo, 2014). To learn more about the legal requirements, consult with a school district bond consultant.

Other Borrowing

One other borrowing option for school districts is the lease-purchase agreement

(Braun, 2022). For school districts without sufficient reserves to purchase certain capital outlay items or which prefer to extend the payment of a large purchase over more than one year, this may be a viable alternative.

The most common uses of lease-purchase agreements are for school busses, copiers, and technology hardware. A school district will enter into a contract with a leasing agent to obtain the funds necessary to purchase needed capital items immediately. As part of the agreement, the district will pay back the loan with interest over several years. This option is especially helpful to financially needy school districts.

SUMMARY

In this chapter, we examined the primary options for short and long-term borrowing. We discussed the debt service extension base, particularly as it relates to school bonds. We studied the five primary long-term bond types including their unique characteristics as well as capital leasing.

Chapter 7

Financial Planning

Now that you are armed with a basic understanding of both the revenue and expenditures sides of the school finance equation, we are ready to discuss a critical element of fiscal management: long-range financial planning. That is, how school administrators plan for the financial health of their school districts.

A good way to conceptualize the process is to relate it to your personal financial planning. Let me begin by asking you to consider several questions.

- Would you buy a new car without considering how you would pay for it?
- Would you buy a home without weighing your relative job security?
- Would you wait until you were 65 before planning for your retirement?
- Would you buy US Savings Bonds exclusively without ever considering other investment options because you had read about them in a government advertisement?
- Would you postpone saving for your children's college educations until the day they graduated from high school?

Of course, you would not. In fact, I am sure you would assess your current and potential income level, evaluate your savings plan, and consider your short and long-term liabilities. You would also begin to speculate about your personal financial future including where your career may take you and what known and unknown factors might await you. As part of this process, you would also make your best guesses on what the next few years may hold; then, as time passes, factor in new information, and adjust your financial planning course. The chances are that because you are a responsible person you would not put on a pair of blinders and just hope everything will magically work out so that you would be free to sail off on a new yacht into the retirement sunset somewhere in the Caribbean free of financial worries!

Successful school district administrators similarly plan for the financial futures of their school districts. That is, they regularly engage in long-term financial planning. The fact of the matter is that a large number of children, families, school district employees, and community members depend on the wisdom, vision, and planning skills of the school district's administration. They expect that the administration will keep abreast of the latest issues, laws, trends, and practices in order to maintain quality educational programs and services, all while keeping the school district as financially solvent as possible. I use "as possible" because even under sound administrative leadership, financial crisis may be inevitable. Administrators sometimes have little or no control over some factors. Yet, for most districts, sound long-range financial planning may be the difference between successful financial problem-solving and crisis management.

LONG-RANGE FINANCIAL PLANNING

What exactly is long-range financial planning? It is a process which central office administrators use to project the long-term financial health of the school district and ultimately make decisions which affect the educational program and services offered. Through a long-range financial planning process, most administrators will look out over the next five years and make their best informed estimate of the future financial position of the school district.

Financial projections must be built on solid data and realistic assumptions to be useful (Kersten & Diaz, 2021). If so, they are usually quite accurate for a year or two. However, because the future is subject to change and projections are primarily forecasts of trends and/or a range of possibilities, they become increasingly imprecise after a couple of years. Even though projections are reasonably valid only for the short-term, prudent administrators know that they must plan for five years in order to ensure that they are taking into consideration as broad a perspective as possible. Otherwise, through short-sighted thinking, they may plunge the district into a financial crisis in a relatively short period of time.

Consider this example. A school district has a reserve of $20M and an annual budget of $40M. At first look, you might say that the school district is very solvent. However, if you look more closely, you may find a different picture. For example, if the school district is experiencing a $3M annual budget deficit and property tax revenue is increasing only at the rate of inflation while other costs including salaries are outstripping inflation by at least 3%, or if the school board is planning to add several new programs while also reducing class size by three students, the $20M reserve will disappear within 5 years. If you had just looked at the current year, you could conclude that the district is financially stable. However, if you considered all information available, your analysis would be much different. It is precisely for this reason that school district administrators must maintain a multi-year perspective if they are to project a relatively accurate picture of the district's financial future.

PREPARING FINANCIAL PROJECTIONS

The process of preparing financial projections begins with the selection of a financial software tool. School administrators typically purchase a commercial product or develop their own which could include a regular spreadsheet. A good way to gather information to help you decide what approach to use is to network with other school business officials or superintendents in your area. They can be a valuable resource to you.

After selecting the tool, the next step is to identify revenue and expenditure assumptions. In order to develop useful projections, you must make some assumptions (informed estimates) of what will happen on the revenue and expenditure sides of the equation over the next few years. The decisions you make during this phase are critical in the projection process. In fact, the more accurate your assumptions are, the more useful your projections. On the other hand, if your assumptions are either too high or low, your projections will be essentially useless and your credibility as a financial manager will be called into question.

As a result, one of the most important responsibilities in financial planning is doing your "homework." Seasoned school business officials know that the recent past is often a good predictor of the near future. Therefore, they gather as much information as possible from the immediate past and combine it with their best estimates of future trends to develop revenue and expenditure assumptions. Typical areas to study include:

- Recent pertinent school district data such as staffing patterns, retirements, enrollment, educational program and facility needs, insurance costs, and collective bargaining agreements;
- Recent statewide data on PTELL levels, state aid support, and unfunded mandates;
- Property tax assessments including new growth and business property tax appeals;
- State and federal funding levels; and,
- Pending state and federal legislation.

In addition, administrators gather as much information as possible from federal and state agencies as well as professional organizations and private sources to thoroughly understand any factors which may impact school funding. Finally, they actively lobby legislators and other key officials who are the educational policy makers. Only through such a thorough and informed inquiry process can school administrators be well prepared to develop sound 5-year financial projections.

To illustrate common financial projection assumptions, I have included below revenue and expenditure assumptions for a sample school district. Later in this chapter, I will use these assumptions as the basis for a set of five-year projections.

- Tax revenues are projected within the constraints of the tax cap and business property tax appeals
- The tax cap is projected at 2.1%
- Equalized Assessed Valuation (EAV) of the District is projected to increase due to new property growth (based on information on new property) and annual reassessment increases of 2%
- Interest revenue is projected at a 2% rate of return on invested reserves
- Lunch, fees and other local revenue are projected to increase 2% per year

- State Aid, CPPTRR, and federal aid are projected to remain constant at a level based on the average of the last 3 years

Sample Expenditure Assumptions

- Enrollment and staffing are projected to remain constant
- Total salary costs are projected to increase 4.0% per year
- Benefit and utility costs are expected to increase 8% per year
- Service cost increases are estimated at 5% per year
- Special education tuition costs are projected to increase 7% per year
- Expendable material and equipment cost increases are held at 4% per year

Earlier in this chapter, I noted that financial projections are relatively accurate for a couple of years. However, since projections are built on assumptions (best guesses) with a goal of showing trends and a range of possibilities, the future is often somewhat different from what is predicted. As a result, financial projections become increasingly imprecise as years pass. If you had some mystical power to know the future, that would be wonderful; but you do not. What you quickly learn through the financial planning process is that you will encounter many unknowns and must regularly adjust your projections to maintain accuracy.

Financial Projections - Operating Funds

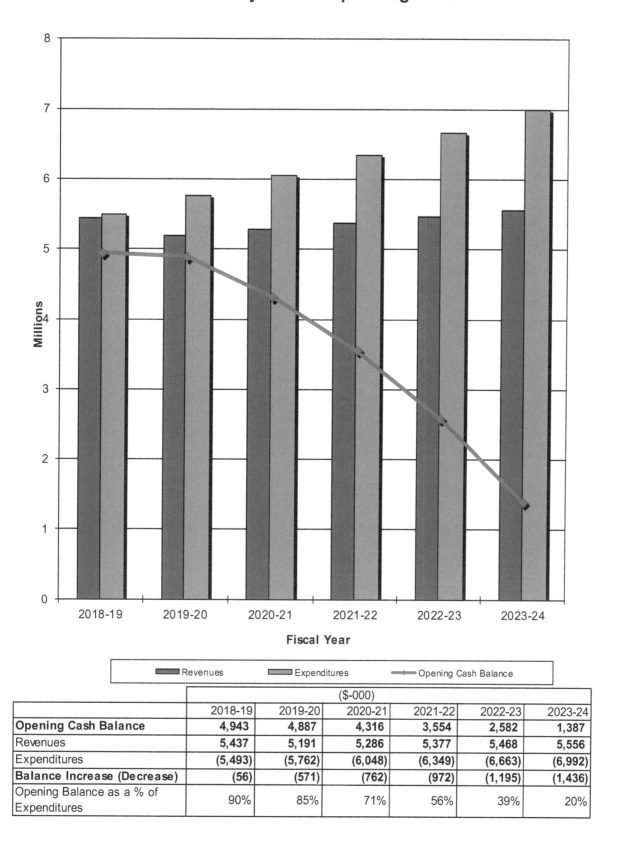

	($-000)					
	2018-19	2019-20	2020-21	2021-22	2022-23	2023-24
Opening Cash Balance	**4,943**	**4,887**	**4,316**	**3,554**	**2,582**	**1,387**
Revenues	**5,437**	**5,191**	**5,286**	**5,377**	**5,468**	**5,556**
Expenditures	**(5,493)**	**(5,762)**	**(6,048)**	**(6,349)**	**(6,663)**	**(6,992)**
Balance Increase (Decrease)	**(56)**	**(571)**	**(762)**	**(972)**	**(1,195)**	**(1,436)**
Opening Balance as a % of Expenditures	90%	85%	71%	56%	39%	20%

Figure 7.1. Five-Year Financial Projection

Before we study the figure above, please note that financial projections exclude the Debt Service Fund since it is outside the tax cap.

In the bar graph, the left bar (dark) represents the revenues and the right (light) expenditures. The line shows the opening cash balance; in other words, the amount of dollars which the district had on July 1 of a particular school year.

You will note that the first year of the projections is the most recent one for which all data are known. It is from this point that school business officials apply their assumptions to project revenues and expenditures for subsequent years.

Let's begin by understanding how to read the bar graph and financial data. On the left hand side of the bar graph are numbers representing dollar levels. At the bottom are the current and projected school years. If you examine FY2019, you see that the school district had revenues (dark bar) of $5,437,000 (5,437M) and expenditures (light bar) of $5,493,000 (5,493M). The trend line shows that the district began the 2018-19 school year with an opening balance of $4,943,000 ($4,943M).

Reading the chart, you also see that the district had an operating deficit that year of $56,000 because expenditures (5,493M) exceeded revenues (($5,437M) by $56,000. Overall, the district's cash balance at the end of FY19 decreased to $4,887M, the amount of the next year's opening balance.

Another way to categorize a district's financial position is to calculate the ratio of the year's opening balance as a percent of the year's expenditures. The higher the figure, the better is the district's financial position.

In Figure 7.1, you see that this school district begins FY20 with $4,887M and anticipates expenditures of $5,762M. To calculate its opening balance as a percent of expenditures, you merely divide $4,887M Opening Cash Balance by $5,762M Expenditures and see that the district begins the FY20 school year with enough reserves to pay 90% of the year's expenditures. For most school districts, this is an enviable position. Before they receive any revenues, they know that they have sufficient reserves to pay more almost three quarters of next year's costs.

Here, though, is where we see the real value of long-term projections. If you just looked at the large cash reserve and the 90% figure, you could conclude that this district has no financial concerns. However, when you begin to factor in the assumptions including the growing deficit over five years, the picture begins to change dramatically.

INTERPRETING THE PROJECTIONS

Now that you can read the projections, let's interpret them. As I approach my projections, I first take a global look at the overall financial picture of the district. Ask yourself this question. When you study the graph, is this a positive or negative financial projection? What I see is a district heading toward financial difficulty. Under the assumptions, expenditures are rising at a much faster rate than revenues as the costs of salaries, benefits, supplies, and services are projected to far exceed the inflation-based revenue increases limited by the tax cap. To understand this, study the salary and expenditure lines across the five projected year. You also note that the line (opening balance) is dropping quickly during the projection period. If the district does not increase revenues or reduce expenditures, between FY 19 and FY24, the district's overall opening balance will have dropped by $3.56M or 72% signaling a pending financial crisis.

The value of projections is that they allow the school district administration and board of education to have time to study the district's financial future and begin to make adjustments now that will improve the long-term outlook. A good rule of thumb is to make as many adjustments as early as possible since the effect of either revenue increases or expenditure reductions is compounded over time. That is, a small change today has a much bigger impact than waiting three years.

A good analogy that may help you understand the power of compounding is to consider what financial planners tell their clients about retirement planning. They always advise people to start savings as soon as possible, preferably in their early twenties rather than waiting until they are in their 40s. They know that this strategy translates into a much higher portfolio value at retirement. In fact, you can actually invest significantly less when you are 20s than if you wait until your 40s and retire with the same or even more funds, primarily because of compounding.

WORKING WITH PROJECTIONS

Financial projections should be used as an ongoing planning tool by school administrators to monitor the financial position of the school district and to assist in decision-making. Experienced administrators typically update financial projections regularly during the year as new information becomes available and present annual projections to the board of education as part of the yearly budget development process.

Administrators can also use financial projections as a planning tool. By altering the revenue and expenditure assumptions or making changes to revenues and/or expenditures, you can test the impact of any actions you are considering prior to recommending them to the board of education.

To illustrate the use of projections as a planning tool, let's study the impact of a one time expenditure reduction coupled with a working cash bond sale can have on the basic projection above. In this scenario, the tax capped school district has an annual debt service extension base of $1.5M. This means that the district can sell $3M in bonds and repay them over two years. Under this approach, they can sell bonds every other year.

Proposed Actions

Listed below are actions that the superintendent and the school business official are considering. The question is - What would be the likely impact on the school district's five-year financial projections if these actions were taken?

Revenue Enhancement

- $500,000 Working Cash Bond Sale Every Two

Years Expenditure Reductions

- $60,000 – One teacher
- $20,000 - Teacher Assistants/Clerical Staff
- $10,000 - Benefits
- $200,000 - Service Reductions
- $15,000 - Supply Reductions

Financial Projections - Operating Funds
With Reductions and Bonds

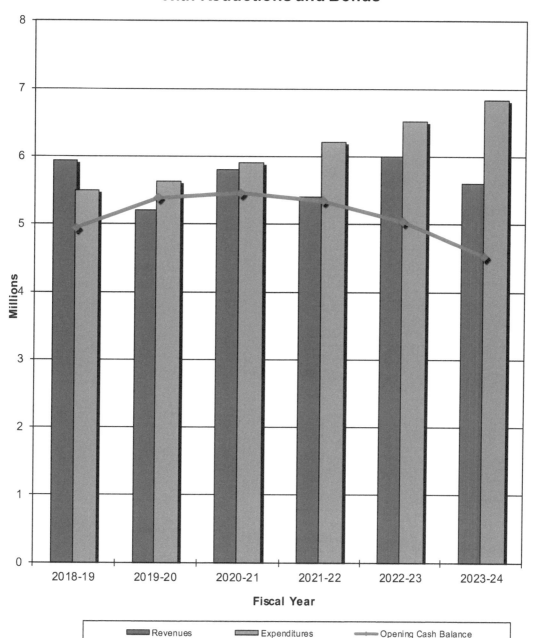

	($-000)					
	2018-19	2019-20	2020-21	2021-22	2022-23	2023-24
Opening Cash Balance	**4,943**	**5,387**	**5,457**	**5,345**	**5,043**	**4,528**
Revenues	5,937	5,202	5,800	5,405	5,999	5,601
Expenditures	(5,493)	(5,632)	(5,912)	(6,207)	(6,514)	(6,837)
Bond Sale		500	-	500	-	500
Balance Increase (Decrease)	**444**	**70**	**(112)**	**(302)**	**(515)**	**(736)**
Opening Balance as a % of Expenditures	90%	96%	92%	86%	77%	66%

Figure 7.2. Five-Year Financial Projection with Proposed Actions

Impact of Proposed Changes. By implementing a $305,000 expenditure reduction and selling $500,000 in working cash bonds every two years, the district would substantially improve its five-year financial picture. The school district opened FY19 with a balance of $4,943M, however, in the original base projections that balance rapidly diminished. By taking the proposed actions, the district would begin FY24 with an opening cash balance of $4,528M rather than $1,387M. Because of the power of compounding and the fact that the district took action immediately rather than waiting until the its financial position approached the crisis stage, the district improved its opening balance position over five years from 20% to 66%. Although you may not be able to increase your revenues substantially, you may may be able to significantly impact your district's financial position by using five-year financial projections as a planning tool.

SUMMARY

Chapter 7 explored the efficacy of financial planning in school district management. Also discussed was the financial planning process, including the development of five-year projections. Finally, we looked at the uses and limitations inherent in school district financial planning as well as the importance of planning for sound fiscal management.

Chapter 8

Personnel

School districts are people businesses. At the risk of pointing out the obvious, the single largest expense in any school district is employee-related. For most school districts, salaries account for 60% or more of all expenditures. Therefore, an important consideration for any district administrator is the cost associated with employees. In this chapter, we will examine how school districts determine staffing levels and employee compensation. We will also look at common employee benefits and retirement systems.

STAFFING PATTERNS

No one approach to staffing is pervasive in Illinois school districts. The reality is that school districts often choose staffing approaches that reflect local factors. Some districts are highly unionized, while others tend to be somewhat paternalistic. In certain instances, parents are very influential in district policy setting; while in others, community groups or teachers have a strong voice in many matters. As a result, issues related to collective bargaining or political forces associated with employee, parent, and community groups will influence how the school board staffs its schools.

Some school districts establish firm staffing ratios either through board policy or collective bargaining agreements. For example, a school board may set a policy which states that no kindergarten class may exceed 23 students; while in others, collective bargaining agreements include class size maximums. Under either approach, if any class section exceeds the cap, the school district adds a new class section.

Other school districts operate under staffing guidelines which do not automatically require the addition of a new class when a section exceeds a maximum enrollment. Rather, the guidelines, which are usually written as administrative procedures, serve as a preferred class size range. Under this model, the administration and school board retain the authority to determine final staffing levels. See a sample of staffing guidelines below (Table 8.1).

The firm staffing ratio method can be problematic for school districts, especially those with limited classroom space or financial concerns, since the addition of a new class section is mandatory. In contrast, staffing guidelines facilitate a thoughtful approach to management without the inflexibility associated with firm maximums. School districts would be well advised to maintain a flexible rather than a firm staffing ratio approach.

Not all school districts have staffing models. In these instances, no specific staffing ratio requirement or guideline exists. For some districts, this approach is effective. Staffing decisions are made by the school board on a case-by-case basis often on the counsel of the district administration or by delegation to the administration. However, the absence of a formal policy or procedures may create some internal or external issues often related to inequities.

Class size issues can become a source of conflict within school districts. It is not unusual for parents and teachers to lobby administrators and school board members, often at open board meetings, to lower class size. Also, controversies periodically emerge when special education students are mainstreamed into regular classes for parts of a school day. The issue usually centers on whether the guidelines should be altered to reflect the partial mainstreaming of special education students. Although staffing ratios or guidelines are no guarantee of political stability, they can provide a structure to help focus discussion.

Table 8.1
Sample Staffing Guidelines

Grade	Range	Maximums	Number of Sections			
			2	3	4	5
Kdg.	15 – 23	23	24 – 46	47 – 69	70 – 92	93 – 115
1	15 – 23	23	24 – 46	47 – 69	70 – 92	93 – 115
2	16 – 24	24	25 – 48	49 – 72	73 – 96	97 – 120
3	16 – 24	24	25 – 48	49 – 72	73 – 96	97 – 120
4	17 – 25	25	26 – 50	51 – 75	76 – 100	101 – 125
5	17 – 25	25	26 – 50	51 – 75	76 – 100	101 – 125

EMPLOYEE COMPENSATION

Employee compensation methods vary from district to district, but to a large extent, they are driven by employee satisfaction. In this section, we will examine each of the three main employee groups individually: teachers, non-certified personnel, and administrators. However, before discussing compensation models, it is important to understand the concept of salary market philosophy.

- Is it fair for teachers to argue that they should be paid more than auto mechanics because they have a higher level of education?
- Do superintendents in a particular geographic area earning an average of $150,000 have a valid point when they argue that they should be paid more since superintendents in another region of the state average $195,000?
- Is it valid for teachers in one district to select the teacher salary schedule from the highest paying district in the state and demand because they are paid the same because they work just as hard?
- Is the school board fair when it contends during the collective bargaining process that their teachers are too highly paid when the Board selectively chose 10 of the lowest paying school districts in the area for comparison?

The answers, of course, are no. Educators, similar to other professions, are compensated commensurate with what other educators are paid within some logically defined market. This market area usually includes some specific geographic boundaries and type of district (K-8, 9-12, or K-12). Often both the teachers and school boards agree to a defined market during the collective bargaining process.

By way of example, in the school district where I served as superintendent, we had an agreement that the "salary market" for teacher compensation included all the elementary and high school districts in three townships: Evanston, New Trier, and Niles. This helped provide focus during the bargaining process

Defining the market is only the first step in the compensation process. The second is establishing a market philosophy by setting a target for employee compensation in the market area. Some districts have clearly defined market positions such as "We want our employees to be paid at the average of the market." Still others may decide that their teachers should be compensated similarly to other high paying districts. Similarly, some may offer significantly higher beginning salaries to attract new more candidates but limit salary levels for more experienced teachers. However, others may not actually define a specific market philosophy directly; however, a review of their salary schedules usually reflects their compensation philosophies.

Teacher Compensation

Even though calls for merit plan plans or performance bonuses are more common than they were years ago, teachers are still paid similar to the way they have been paid for decades. That is, they are compensated through teacher salary schedules with salary increases based on experience (steps) and the number of semester graduate credits (lanes) earned. The number of steps and lanes vary, however, from district to district and are usually determined through the collective bargaining process. They are also influenced heavily by the financial position of the school district since a lack of resources may limit the increase the board of education is willing to accept. A sample school district FY 2022-23 teacher salary schedule follows:

TEACHERS' SALARY SCHEDULE 2022-23

Steps		BA		BA+16		MA		MA+8		MA+16		MA+24		MA+32
	Index	Amount	Index	Amount	Index	Amount	Index	Amount	Index	Amount	Index	Amount	Index	Amount
1	1.00	46,351	1.050	48,669	1.12	51,913	1.14	52,840	1.16	53,767	1.18	54,694	1.20	55,621
2	1.03	47,742	1.080	50,059	1.16	53,767	1.18	54,694	1.20	55,621	1.22	56,548	1.24	57,475
3	1.08	50,059	1.120	51,913	1.21	56,085	1.23	57,012	1.25	57,939	1.27	58,866	1.29	59,793
4	1.13	52,377	1.170	54,231	1.26	58,402	1.28	59,329	1.30	60,256	1.32	61,183	1.34	62,110
5	1.18	54,694	1.220	56,548	1.31	60,720	1.33	61,647	1.35	62,574	1.37	63,501	1.39	64,428
6	1.22	56,548	1.270	58,866	1.37	63,501	1.39	64,428	1.41	65,355	1.43	66,282	1.45	67,209
7	1.27	58,866	1.310	60,720	1.43	66,282	1.45	67,209	1.47	68,136	1.49	69,063	1.51	69,990
8	1.31	60,720	1.350	62,574	1.49	69,063	1.51	69,990	1.53	70,917	1.55	71,844	1.57	72,771
9	1.34	62,110	1.390	64,428	1.55	71,844	1.57	72,771	1.59	73,698	1.61	74,625	1.63	75,552
10	1.37	63,501	1.420	65,818	1.61	74,625	1.63	75,552	1.65	76,479	1.67	77,406	1.69	78,333
11	1.40	64,891	1.450	67,209	1.67	77,406	1.69	78,333	1.71	79,260	1.73	80,187	1.75	81,114
12	1.43	66,282	1.480	68,599	1.73	80,187	1.75	81,114	1.77	82,041	1.79	82,968	1.81	83,895
13	1.45	67,209	1.510	69,990	1.79	82,968	1.81	83,895	1.83	84,822	1.85	85,749	1.87	86,676
14	1.47	68,136	1.540	71,381	1.85	85,749	1.87	86,676	1.89	87,603	1.91	88,530	1.93	89,457
15	1.48	68,599	1.570	72,771	1.92	88,994	1.94	89,921	1.96	90,848	1.98	91,775	2.00	92,702
16	1.49	69,063	1.585	73,466	1.94	89,921	1.96	90,848	1.98	91,775	2.00	92,702	2.02	93,629
17	1.50	69,527	1.600	74,162	1.96	90,848	1.98	91,775	2.00	92,702	2.02	93,629	2.04	94,556
18	1.51	69,990	1.615	74,857	1.98	91,775	2.00	92,702	2.02	93,629	2.04	94,556	2.06	95,483
19	1.52	70,454	1.630	75,552	2.00	92,702	2.02	93,629	2.04	94,556	2.06	95,483	2.08	96,410
20	1.53	70,917	1.645	76,247	2.02	93,629	2.04	94,556	2.06	95,483	2.08	96,410	2.10	97,337
21	1.54	71,381	1.660	76,943	2.04	94,556	2.06	95,483	2.08	96,410	2.10	97,337	2.12	98,264
22	1.55	71,844	1.675	77,638	2.06	95,483	2.08	96,410	2.10	97,337	2.12	98,264	2.14	99,191
23	1.56	72,308	1.690	78,333	2.08	96,410	2.10	97,337	2.12	98,264	2.14	99,191	2.16	100,118
24	1.57	72,771	1.705	79,028	2.10	97,337	2.12	98,264	2.14	99,191	2.16	100,118	2.18	101,045
25	1.58	73,235	1.720	79,724	2.12	98,264	2.14	99,191	2.16	100,118	2.18	101,045	2.20	101,972
26	1.59	73,698	1.735	80,419	2.14	99,191	2.16	100,118	2.18	101,045	2.20	101,972	2.22	102,899
27	1.60	74,162	1.750	81,114	2.16	100,118	2.18	101,045	2.20	101,972	2.22	102,899	2.24	103,826
28	1.61	74,625	1.765	81,810	2.18	101,045	2.20	101,972	2.22	102,899	2.24	103,826	2.26	104,753
29	1.62	75,089	1.780	82,505	2.20	101,972	2.22	102,899	2.24	103,826	2.26	104,753	2.28	105,680
30	1.63	75,552	1.795	83,200	2.22	102,899	2.24	103,826	2.26	104,753	2.28	105,680	2.30	106,607

You probably noticed that along the left side there are 30 steps. Teachers move up one step each year. This is what is referred to as the step increase. One source of confusion and sometimes disagreement in collective bargaining relates to the step increase. Traditionally, teachers do not equate a step change to a raise while school board members do. The reality is that step movement is a raise because it increases a teacher's salary from one year to the next. Even if the salary schedule as a whole did not change, teachers would still receive higher salaries the following year as they moved up a step. Only those at step 30 would not see an increase.

During presentations to the board of education or during contract negotiations, you will hear the term, average cost of step. As part of the budget preparation process or during collective bargaining, school business officials will calculate the average cost of the step increase. This figure represents the average percentage increase to the board for all teachers. It is not uncommon for an average cost of a step increase to be 2% or more. Therefore, without any salary schedule increase, teachers will average 2% higher salaries merely because they moved up a step on the teacher salary schedule.

In addition to steps, teachers' salaries increase if they earn additional graduate study credit. You will notice that our sample teacher salary schedule has seven lanes ranging from BA to MA+32. The number of lanes varies significantly from district to district; however, they too have additional salary increases associated with them.

Therefore, teachers who move up a step and earn enough graduate course credit to change lanes would receive raises for both even if the schedule stayed the same.

To illustrate this further, let's take a look at the percentage increase a teacher would receive on our sample schedule even if the schedule remained the same from year to year. For calculation purposes, here are our assumptions.

- Teacher moved from BA Step 4 to MA Step 5; and,
- The salary schedule as a whole remained the same

Table 8.2
Salary Increase Cost Comparison

FY 2023 Salary	FY 2024 Salary	Salary Increase	Salary Increase
$52,377	$60,720	$8,343	15.9%

Isn't this interesting? This particular teacher would receive a 15.9% increase without any schedule change. The FY2024 salary would even be higher if the entire salary schedule increased.

Finally, you may also be familiar with the term "schedule increase." Traditionally, teacher schedules in their entirety increase annually. When the complete schedule increases, this is referred to as a schedule increase.

Most teachers actually receive at least two separate annual increases: schedule and step. Some also qualify for a lane-related increase if they earn additional graduate course credit. Is it any wonder that when contract negotiations heat up and percent increase figures are discussed by the Board and teachers as well as written about in local newspapers that there is some confusion?

In addition to the steps and lanes on our sample schedule, you also see something called the index. Many but not all salary schedules are built on indexes. When salary schedules are distributed to teachers, sometimes the indexes are not included because they can be a source of confusion for those not familiar with salary schedule structures. What most teachers really want to know is – "What is my salary for the year"?

Administrators need to understand salary schedule indexing. In the schedule above, the index represents the percentage that any point on the salary schedule is higher than the base (BA Step1) salary. To illustrate this, look at BA Step I. The salary for this step is $46,351. BA Step 2 has an index of 1.03. To calculate the salary for BA Step 2, you multiple the base salary $46,351 by the index for the step (1.03) resulting in a BA Step 2 salary of $47,742.

$46,351 X 1.03 = $47,742

The same process is used to establish each point on the salary schedule. One advantage of this system is that a district can negotiate a base salary then create a spreadsheet with built in indexes to almost instantly create a salary schedule.

A salary schedule indexing system can provide valuable insights into a school district's salary philosophy. If you study the indexing pattern in Teachers' Salary Schedule 2022-23, what conclusion might you draw about this school district's salary philosophy? Here are a few that I would suggest. The school district:

- Encourages teachers to earn their masters degree. Note the large increase in index points between the BA+16 and MA lanes.
- Encourages increased educational training up to the MA level but does not value it as much beyond that since index point increases are much smaller.
- Strives to increase teachers' salaries more quickly during their first 15 years, possibly to achieve earlier comparability in the market area. Beyond that point, index points only increase .01 to .02 annually.
- Encourages employee longevity. Not only does it have a 30 step scale, but the top salary is substantial.

You may want to examine your own district's salary schedule to see what patterns you can identify.

Another common feature of teacher compensation programs is the inclusion of longevity provisions. These are usually additional salary amounts, which are added to teachers' salaries the year after they have reached the last step on the schedule. These are established during the collective bargaining process and are generally listed as a footnote on the salary schedule. If, for example, the district teacher salary schedule above had a $500 per year longevity provision, a teacher with 31 years of service in the MA32 lane would be paid $107,107. Longevity increases are cumulative and continue as long as the teacher is employed.

Finally, it is important to recognize that not only does the teacher salary schedule approach have a long history in public education, but the Illinois state legislature has all but ensured that the present model will continue with passage of the Illinois Educational Labor Relations Act of 1984. This law requires school boards to bargain collectively with teacher unions. In essence, it narrows the compensation model options by requiring agreement from teachers before any change can be made in teacher salaries (Braun, 2022).

Emerging Trends in Teacher Compensation

As noted earlier, teachers generally continue to be compensated based on traditional salary schedules. However, a few years ago, new compensation models began to emerge. One was negotiating two-tiered salary schedules. Typically, this involved agreeing to a separate and lower salary schedule for new teachers while continuing the higher schedule for other teachers. Districts such as Arlington Heights School District 25 and Palatine School District 15 are examples of this compensation approach.

Another negotiations focus has been on what was once unthinkable, the elimination of the traditional teacher salary schedule. Examples of school districts which have eliminated the traditional teacher salary schedule include Skokie School District 69, Wilmette 39, Golf 67, Morton Grove 70, and Skokie 73. Teachers now receive percentage increases tied to their prior year salary. At the moment, these approaches hare receiving less attention than they did a few years ago. However, an important question to consider is – Will these teacher compensation approaches become more prevalent or slowly disappear through the collective bargaining process?

Non-Certified Personnel

Non-certified personnel (support staff) compensation models tend to be less structured than those of teachers. Even though they enjoy the same collective bargaining rights as teachers, a smaller percent of support staff groups tends to form unions. Historically, they have not sought the same level of unionization as teachers. They also tend to be smaller groups, which were not initially as universally organized as were teachers by national level associations such as the American Federation of Teachers or the National Education Association. Support staff may either affiliate with teachers' unions or form their own.

Although some school districts compensate support staff using a salary schedule model, others are paid primarily on an hourly basis or through some version of a merit-based plan. Others receive annual salaries not tied directly to schedules. Therefore, you will find a variety of compensation models, often primarily a function of local past practices and tradition.

Finally, one common misunderstanding among school administrators is that salaried support staff members are exempt from the overtime pay provisions of the Fair Labor Standards Act. Even if employees are salaried, they are entitled to overtime pay unless they meet the legal standards for exempt status (Braun, 2022).

Administrative Compensation

In Illinois, administrators are management. As such, their salaries are set at the discretion of the board of education. For the most part, administrators need an Illinois administrative licensure. However, certain employees in some districts, such as psychologists or deans of students, are not part of a bargaining unit nor required to hold an administrative licensure. They may, however, be compensated under the administrative classification.

Administrative compensation models vary from school district to school district. Several of the most common approaches are discussed below.

Administrative Salary Schedules. Although Illinois administrators are not permitted to bargain collectively because they are classified as management employees, school boards may choose to cooperate with administrators as a group as occurs in Chicago 299. Under this approach, a salary schedule model is used to establish compensation by administrative positions.

Across the Board Increases. Another common compensation model is some form of across the board salary increases. Sometimes the percentage increase is equal to that of other employee groups. Under this approach, administrators typically receive the same percentage increase given to other employee groups such as teachers. However, even with an across the board model, it is not uncommon for boards of education to make exceptions for certain administrators who are viewed as underpaid. The term "catch up" is used to describe a special additional one-time salary increase.

Merit Increases. Unlike teachers, administrators may be compensated under some version of a merit pay plan. Whether this takes the form of linking administrators' salary increases to performance indicators or the awarding of a bonus, merit plans tend to be individual in nature. In many instances, actual salary increases under merit plans may be tied to meeting broad goals or even the reputation of the administrator as perceived by the board of education and/or superintendent rather than exact quantitative criteria. Nonetheless, this model is common in Illinois.

Unique Plans. In addition to the above approaches, school boards may adopt any other compensation model they choose. In one district in which I served, administrators were paid based upon their position in the salary market. The compensation philosophy was to pay administrators toward the low end of the salary market range for their position when they were hired. Then, as they performed satisfactorily over a number of years, their salaries would increase to the point that they ultimately reached the third quartile of their market.

Quartile refers to the position of the salary in the market. For example, if you had a market composed of 19 administrators whose salaries were ranked from the bottom to the top. The 5th salary from the bottom would be the 1st quartile, the 10th would represent the second quartile or median while the 15th would be the 3rd quartile. Therefore, at the 3rd quartile, three-quarters of the salaries in the market would be lower.

Under this model, each year an administrator's salary would be compared to a quartile distribution for that position in the market. Any administrator at the 3rd quartile of their market would receive a market-based increase. Those who fell below the 3rd quartile would receive an additional "catch up" increase depending upon their market position. For example, if an administrator's salary fell in the 1st quartile (the lowest salary up to the first quartile), the person would receive an additional 3% salary increase. From the 1st quartile to the 2nd quartile or median, the increase would be 2%; while above the median to the 3rd quartile, the salary raise would increase 1%. However, if an administrator's salary exceeded the 3rd quartile, the person would have 1% deducted from the market increase since the compensation philosophy goal was to pay administrators at the 3rd quartile of the market.

Through this process, administrators were well paid but not the highest. Since the system was market data-driven versus arbitrary, it was perceived by administrators as fair and equitable. It is also important to note that the superintendent could recommend a smaller or even no raise for any administrator not performing to district standards.

EMPLOYEE BENEFITS

Frequently, the second largest reoccurring district expenditure is for employee benefits. It is not unusual for benefit costs to be 10% or more of overall expenditures. This is not surprising since one of the widely recognized advantages of a career in public education has traditionally been excellent benefits.

The most common general employee benefits include:

1. Insurance
   a. Health
   b. Dental
   c. Vision
   d. Term life
   e. Disability

2. Paid Time Off
   a. Sick days
   b. Personal or business days
   c. Vacation: administrators and non-certified employees

Depending upon the employee group, these benefits may vary. Most often, requiring employees to pay at least a portion of any insurance premium is considered sound policy. Without some cost, employees may automatically accept a benefit even if it is not needed, thereby driving up district costs. For example, employees may be covered by their spouses' health insurance plans, but also take advantage of the district's insurance if offered at no cost. Under the other hand, if employees have to pay a portion of the premium, they may elect to decline district coverage.

Another advantage of shared premium costs is that it encourages employee groups to participate in studying ways to reduce premiums (Kersten & Dada, 2005). School districts may collaborate with employees to form committees designed to study insurance programs in order to find ways to reduce costs while maintaining acceptable coverage levels. Since both the district and employees benefit from premium reductions, this can be a win-win situation for both. In times of tight finances, school districts are wise to look for such strategies to reduce overall benefit costs.

HEALTH CARE OPTIONS

Do you remember the first time you were asked to select from an array of healthcare plans? If you are similar to many employees, you were probably confused. You may have had to choose from a list of options ranging from traditional fee for service plans to health maintenance organization (HMO) with varying benefit and premium cost levels. Although an in-depth understanding of each may be necessary for school business officials, what you really need is a basic understanding of the various options. In this section, I will summarize the key elements of each. To fully understand the differences in your local school district plans including options even within the categories below, you will want to contact the school district's insurance specialist.

Health Maintenance Organization

Usually the lowest cost healthcare plan for both the school district and the employee is the HMO. Often referred to as a managed care plan, participants select a primary care physician within the Health Maintenance Organization (HMO) network who initiates medical treatment as necessary which may include referral to HMO approved specialist as needed. The primary advantages of an HMO include:

- Lower premiums;
- No deductibles;
- Low co-pays for services; and,
- No claim filing paperwork.

Because of the reduced costs, those electing an HMO lose the flexibility to receive treatment from medical professionals not part of the HMO network (Kersten & Dada, 2005).

Preferred Provider Option

A most popular employee insurance option is the Preferred Provider Option (PPO) (Kaiser Family Foundation, 2022). Unlike the HMO, PPOs allow employees to seek medical treatment directly from any healthcare professionals, including specialists, who are part of the PPO network. For this flexibility, those electing the PPO can expect higher annual deductibles and increased out-of-pocket costs. Also, participants must ensure that the doctors they choose are approved by the PPO or be willing to pay substantially more for medical care. However, in most areas, the number of doctors participating in PPOs is usually quite high (Kersten & Dada, 2005).

Fee for Services

A health insurance option which is disappearing from the market is the traditional Fee for Services plan. Under this option, employees have complete freedom of choice for both doctors and hospitals but must complete claim paperwork. However, the high cost of premiums in many districts has eliminated this as an option.

Flexible Spending Accounts and Dependent Care Assistance Plans

Most school districts allow employees to take advantage of an Internal Revenue Service approved option to shelter a portion of their income with a specific limit from federal and state taxes to pay for specific healthcare costs including health insurance premiums, medical and dental care including prescriptions and even certain over-the-counter items through a Flexible Spending Account (FSA). Employees can contribute up to $3,050 (National Institute of Health, 2023). One word of caution. Employees can either rollover up to $500 to the next year or use the amount within 14.5 months of the annual PSA period, otherwise they "lose" it.

A Dependent Care Flexible Spending Account (DCFSA) allows employees to shelter up to $5,000 annually for childcare costs. These funds must be used within 12 months (National Institute of Health, 2023).

Health Reimbursement Account

School districts are also authorized to offer a Health Reimbursement Account (HRA) to employees. This benefit option, which is a specified dollar amount provided by the Board of Education, is usually negotiated as part of collective bargaining. Similar to FSAs, employees may use these tax free funds to pay healthcare costs. School districts often provide these as a way to provide an incentive to participants to accept higher deductibles accompanied by annual lower premiums. Since the lower premium costs benefit both the board and employees while allowing participants to use their HRA to pay the increased deductibles, they can be a win-win for everyone (Kersten & Dada, 2005).

Health Savings Account

An increasingly popular insurance-related benefit is the Health Savings Account (HSA). Although it is probably not appropriate for those who require regular medical care such as families with children or those with high levels of healthcare needs, employees who do not seek healthcare very often may find it attractive. What distinguishes an HSA from a FSA and HRA is that it is actually owned and controlled by the employee, not the school district but is managed through the district. Consequently, participants may carry over HSA funds indefinitely. They are also free to invest HSA funds in a wide range of options including mutual funds. HSAs are typically funded by employees and/or school districts with tax free dollars. (Kersten & Dada, 2005). HSAs must also be offered in conjunction with a regular healthcare plan with deductible minimums for 2023 of $1,500 for single and $3,000 for family coverage. This amount is now annually indexed to inflation (Healthcare.gov, 2023).

REDUCING HEALTH CARE COSTS

As school districts struggle to find ways to reduce expenditures, they often look toward healthcare costs, which traditionally increase at a rate exceeding inflation. Over the last five years, the average premium for family coverage has increased 22%, which is significantly more than the rate of inflation. However, during this time, deductibles and copay have increased much more quickly. In fact, the average deductible has increased 68% over the last ten years. The Kaiser Family Foundation (2022) reports that the average family premium last year was $22,463 or 1.1% more than prior year. The single premium increased by 2.2% to $7,911. Even though the annual rate of increase has slowed, it is still important for school administrators to look for ways to reduce health insurance related costs. Several strategies a colleague and I proposed included the following (Kersten & Dada, 2005).

Telemedicine

A growing trend in the delivery of health care services is telemedicine, which gained momentum during the pandemic. It offers promise to reduce medical costs while providing more convenient access to medical care. A key question yet to be answered is whether this trend is temporary or permanent.

Educate Yourself on Costs

An important first step is learning as much as possible about all aspects of health insurance. Without a sound understanding of healthcare components and costs, little substantial progress can be made.

Analyze Premium Expenditures and Identify Areas for Cost Containment

Since most administrators are not insurance experts, they must rely on industry experts for advice on ways to contain costs. As a result, some consult their present insurance cooperative manager or insurance broker or employ a cost reduction specialist with a high level of industry expertise who will study such areas as:
- Present plan performance;
- Prescription drug program;
- Cost-containment opportunities with employee groups; and,
- Opportunities to negotiate commissions/fixed fees, direct medical services, and claim management.

Partner with Employees

Since both employers and employees benefit from reduction in premium costs, a good starting point for school administrators is to suggest the formation of a joint administration/employee benefit committee led by an insurance consultant to review the current health insurance program and recommend changes that may reduce costs without significantly reducing benefits.

Manage Prescription Plans Aggressively

Prescription drug costs represent a substantial portion of total healthcare costs and are one of the greatest challenges facing employers and employees. Over the past 20 years, Medicare Part D drugs have increased more than twice the rate of inflation (The Commonwealth Fund, 2022). In 2021, US prescription drug costs per person averaged $1,011 (NiceRx, 2023). With the recent dramatic increase in the US inflation rate, prescription drug costs for both employees and employers are only likely to increase further. At the same time, employees are seeing their deductibles rise more rapidly than they have in recent years. As a result, it is important school leaders to continually reassess their healthcare plan and look for ways to reduce costs wherever possible.

Promote Healthier Lifestyles

School administrators may be able to reduce insurance costs by promoting life-style changes. Although the results may not be immediate, they may have an effect over a longer period of time. Some suggestions include:

- Providing wellness screening;
- Offering smoking cessation programs;
- Providing incentives for weight loss and smoking cessation;
- Working with fitness clubs to provide membership specials;
- Sponsoring fitness activities;
- Communicating disease management information; and,
- Highlighting the wellness features of healthcare plans.

OTHER EMPLOYEES INSURANCE OFFERINGS

In addition to health insurance, school district employees may offer several other insurance-related benefits including dental, vision, life, and disability. Premium and benefit levels are typically locally determined, often as an outcome of the collective bargaining process. Dental insurance generally provides full coverage for cleaning while both dental and vision plans pay a percentage of related medical costs. Life insurance usually provided upon death a flat dollar amount or a percentage related to income level. Finally, employees who elect disability insurance are provided a percentage of their income for an extended period when they are unable to work due to illness or injury.

In addition to these insurance benefits, school leaders report offering some less common voluntary benefits with no district costs (Kersten & Diaz, 2021). These include:

- Supplemental individual disability;
- Legal services:
- Identity theft protection;
- Automobile insurance;
- Homeowner/renter insurance; and,
- Pet insurance.

PAID TIME OFF

Finally, a true benefit of a career in education in contrast to the business world is the number of workdays. A widely recognized benefit whether you are an administrator, teacher, or support person is the increased number of days off. Not only do school district employees receive additional paid holidays, but many have extended time off during winter, spring, and summer breaks. Also, school employees are provided generous paid sick leave allocations, often accompanied by unlimited unused sick leave accumulation. It is also common for school districts to allow employees two or more days annually for either personal and/or business use. Twelve month administrators and classified personnel usually receive vacation days in addition to regular school holidays.

BENEFIT PLAN VARIANCES

One area in which administrators are often rewarded beyond other employee groups is in fringe benefits. As with compensation, fringe benefit levels are traditionally tied to an administrative benefit market. Because administrators are usually the smallest employee group and represent the board of education, they typically receive higher board subsidies for insurance premiums, in many instances 100%. In addition, administrators may also be provided travel allowances and conference cost reimbursements not generally available to other employee groups.

Most school district attorneys will recommend that the board of education establish a separate written administrative benefit plan to clearly delineate all fringe benefits. This approach not only establishes a clear understanding of benefits offered but provides continuity during times of administrator and board transition.

TOTAL COMPENSATION

Employees often view total compensation models as equitable since all employees receive the same dollar amount, irrespective of their personal situations. Everyone is treated the same, unlike traditional benefit plans where some employees receive a great deal more in fringe benefit dollars from the district based on their benefit choices. If, for example, a teacher's spouse has a benefit plan that provides family health insurance, the teacher may choose to use the district's fringe benefit dollars for additional salary or a 403(b).

The negative aspect of total compensation for employees is that they assume the risk of premium increases much more directly. Also, insurance premiums often increase at a much greater rate than salaries. As a result, teachers over time may find a larger portion of their pay allocated to pay insurance premiums.

For school district boards, a total compensation approach can be attractive since it places a greater portion of the risk for premium increases on the shoulders of the employees. Also, district costs are more predictable since benefit amounts are fixed.

RETIREMENT PLANS

One of the most substantial public employee benefits is access to a defined benefit retirement plan – lifetime retirement income. Unlike the business world, which has shifted to a defined contribution model such as a 401(k), an investment account owned by the individual employee into which typically both the employee and business contribute, most public school employees still have traditional pension plans. As a result, employees often earn generous lifetime annuities. The three public school retirement systems in Illinois are: Teachers' Retirement System (TRS), Chicago Teachers Pension Fund (CTPF), and Illinois Municipal Retirement Fund (IMRF).

Teachers' Retirement System (TRS)

School district personnel who are required to hold Illinois certification for their positions, including administrators, are members of TRS, which provides three separate pension plans: Tier I, Tier II, and Tier III. For the most part, the plan under which specific employees participate is determined by when they were first hired into any Illinois retirement program. Both Tier I and Tier II are substantially funded by the State of Illinois. No state funds are currently allocated for Tier III plans. However, school districts contribute a small percentage to both Tier I and II. Employees also contribute a portion of their income to help fund each of the three programs (Teachers' Retirement System, 2023).

Tier I

To qualify for Tier I, an employee must have worked in one of the state pension systems prior to January 1, 2011. Under Tier I, both employers and employees contribute a percentage linked to employee salaries. The FY2024 contribution rate for employees is 9.0% of gross salary, while employers contribute 0.58%. In addition, TRS members also contributed an additional 0.90% and employers 0.67% to help subsidize the Teachers' Health Insurance Security (THIS) Fund. TRS participants are eligible to retire at age 60 under the regular program with 10 years of service and at 62 with 5 years. Retirement may occur before age 60, however, the retiree may receive a substantial pension reduction. This will be discussed further later in this section.

TRS is a formula driven system through which retirement annuities are calculated based on a person's years of service and final average salary. For most teachers, the formula is fairly simple. For each year of employment, teachers earn 2.2% in service credit. Therefore, teachers who retire with 20 years of service have accrued service credit of 44% toward the pension formula. If they retire with 35 or more years, they receive the maximum service credit of 75%.

After calculating the service credit percentage, a final average salary is determined by taking the salaries of the highest four consecutive years in the teacher's final ten years and dividing it by four. For example, if the employee's final four highest consecutive salaries were $69,000, $71,000, $73,000, and $75,000, the average annual salary would be $72,000.

Once the percentage and average final salary are calculated, the math is quite simple. However, in order to retire without a penalty, teachers need to either be 60 years of age or have at least 35 full years of service credit. It is important to note that TRS employees may accumulate up to 340 unused and uncompensated sick days for up to two years of service credit (Teachers' Retirement System, 2023).

To illustrate a simple pension calculation, let's assume the teacher:

- Is 60 years old at retirement (No penalty calculation required)
- Has 30 years of service
- Had an average final salary of $75,000

The formula is:

Percentage Earned for Years of Service X Average Final Salary = Annual Pension

66% (.66) X $75,000 = $47,500

Retirees receive a 3% pension increase each January. However, retirees do not begin collecting the 3% increase until the January following their 61st birthday. The good news, though, is that the increase is retroactive to the date of retirement. As a result, many retirees receive a significant pension increase at that time.

Retiring Before 60 with Less Than 35 Years of Service

A question to consider is – what impact does retiring before 60 with less than 35 years of service have on a person's pension? Unfortunately, the effect is substantial. Retirees are subject to a steep pension reduction of 1/2 percent per month (six percent a year) for each month they are under 60. For example, if a person who would otherwise have a pension of $50K retires at age 55, a 30% penalty is applied resulting in an annual pension of $35K. Such a sizable pension reduction may minimize the viability of early retirement.

Salary Increase Maximums

One other provision, which is important to consider, is that there is a maximum amount a person's salary can increase during the final four years of employment without the board of education accruing a substantial penalty. The limit is 6% a year. Boards of education are very reluctant to approve any teacher or administrator contracts, which exceed this level.

Optional Credit

Another important TRS provision you should be aware of is optional service credit. TRS members may earn service credit even when not working in a teacher certified position in an Illinois public school. TRS members may earn service credit for such experiences as military service, employer-approved leaves of absence related to such reasons as childbirth, and certain out-of-state teaching.

Survivor Benefit

As part of their TRS contributions, members pay for survivor benefits. Under this TRS provision, spouses of retirees who have died can elect to receive one-half of the deceased member's pension as well as the 3% annual increases for life.

In this section, we examined a typical, non-complex retirement calculation. However, a full discussion of all possible factors is unrealistic. To understand the system in greater detail or relate it to your personal situation, you are encouraged to either visit the TRS website at http://trsil.org or call their office.

Tier II

Certificated personnel hired after January 1, 2011, are not eligible for Tier I but rather Tier II. Tier II retirees can expect significantly lower retirement benefits than those who retired under Tier 1. Although the impact of these changes is a long way off for most new hires, an understanding of future retirement benefits is essential for long-term financial planning.

The key changes for Tier II include:

- Full benefits beginning at age 67 rather than age 60;
- An option to retire at 62 but with a 6% pension discount for every year under age 67;
- The use of the highest consecutive 8 years salaries for the average salary portion of the pension calculation;
- A maximum final average salary, which is capped at $123.489.18 for FY24, increases annually in step with the CPI. Employees contribute 9% on only income up the the final average salary cap;
- An annual, non-compounded cost of living increase of one half of the CPI but not more than 3%;
- A 66% survivor benefit level; and,
- Tighter post-retirement restrictions on employment in any of the reciprocal systems (Teachers' Retirement System, 2023).

Tier III

In early July 2017, the General Assembly created a new voluntary Tier III pension option. Under plan provisions, all new employees will automatically be enrolled in Tier III unless they purposely select Tier II.

Tier III consists of two parts: a small defined benefit pension (DB) and a defined contribution plan (DC), which is similar to a 403(b). Below is a summary of plan components.

- Members contribute a maximum of 6.2% payroll contribution tied to the cost of their benefits for the DB component.

- Members contribute a minimum of 4% to the DC component.

- The age at retirement is pegged to the normal Social Security retirement age.

- The final average salary for the BD is the employee's salary average for last 10 years of service.

- The automatic pension increase is one-half of the previous year's consumer price index, which is not compounded. There is no maximum percent increase.

81

- The DB pension formula calculation is: number of years of service X 1.25 percent X average annual salary.

- Primary responsibility for funding Tier III falls to individual school districts. However, the State will contribute startup funds during the initial three years (Teachers' Retirement System, 2023).

At the present time, no additional action has been taken on Tier III However, monitoring any potential legislative action would be prudent..

CHICAGO TEACHERS PENSION FUND (CTPF)

The CTPF is similar in many respects to TRS including the formula-driven retirement calculation which uses salary and service credit to determine the actual pension (Chicago Teacher Pension Fund, 2023). However, there are some significant differences. These include:

- A pension contribution of 2% of base salary from the employee and 7% from the Chicago Board of Education;
- Final average salaries used for pension calculation capped at 120% of last year's salary;
- Retirement eligibility at 55 with 20 years of service and a reduced pension;
- A maximum of 244 unused, uncompensated sick days toward service credit;
- At the present time, the Chicago Public School District 299 Board of Education does not offer ERO. The last time it was available, CPS teachers could retire without a reduced pension if they were at least 55 and had 20 years of service;
- The option to retire at age 60 without a reduced pension with a minimum of 20 years of service credit; and,
- A non-retroactive 3% annual compounded pension increase, which begins one year after retirement or 61, whichever occurs later.

The list above summarizes some of the most significant differences. To understand the CTPF provisions more fully, you can access their website at http://ctpf.org or contact their Chicago office.

ILLINOIS MUNICIPAL RETIREMENT FUND (IMRF)

School employees who are not required to hold an Illinois teaching certificate and work 600 or more hours a year for at least 8 years are eligible for an IMRF pension (Illinois Municipal Retirement Fund, 2023). It is interesting to note that this is a state endorsed independent pension system, which also includes other municipal workers such as city and park district employees. Only the employer and employee, not the state, contribute to IMRF.

The minimum retirement age is 55. Employees who retire between 55 and 60 with less than 30 years of service have their pensions reduced by 1/4% for each month they are under 60. If they have 35 years of service but less than 40, their pensions are reduced the lesser of 1/4% per month under age 60 or 1/4% per month under 35 years of service.

Under IMRF, employees' pensions are calculated similar to TRS through a formula which includes two factors: a service credit percentage determined by an employee's experience and an average salary based on the highest consecutive 48 months in the employee's final ten years. Similar to TRS, retirees receive a life-long pension.

Employees contribute 4.5% of their income, while the employer's payment is actuarially determined by IMRF. Members may also use one year of accrued uncompensated sick leave (240 days) for service credit.

An employee's pension can vary significantly based on years of IMRF experience, age at retirement, and salary history. However, to illustrate how the pension formula works, let's consider an employee who has:

- 40 years of service (Number of years of service needed for a maximum pension of 75% of average salary)
- An average annual salary of $50,000 (Average annual salary based on the highest 48 consecutive months in the last 10 years)

The pension formula is:

- Percentage accrued for years of service X Average final salary = Annual Pension
- 75% (.75) X $50,000 = $38,000 Annual Pension

In addition, three other provisions are worth noting. First, a retiree's spouse receives one half of the retiree's pension for life in the event of death. Also, a 3% pension increase tied to the retiree's initial retirement annuity is added each January following retirement.

Retirees also receive additional annual compensation under what IMRF calls the 13th check program. The June 2022 13th payment was approximately 23.602% of the monthly pension. The amount varies from year to year but was designed to partially offset the fixed annual pension increase, which is not cumulative as it is under TRS. IMRF employers contribute a percentage of their payrolls as part of their annual rate to fund this payment. To calculate the retiree payment, IMRF takes the total amount contributed by employers and divides it by the June benefit payments to retirees (Illinois Municipal Retirement Fund, 2023). To understand in greater detail these provisions as well as how an IMRF pension is calculated including the percentage rates for various years of service, please see the fund's website at http://www.imrf.org.

RECIPROCAL SYSTEMS

Under the Illinois Retirement Reciprocal Act, retirees from 11 different systems may combine service credit toward retirement (State of Illinois, 2023). This provision allows, for example, teachers who earn service credit under IMRF as teacher assistants to combine this with their TRS credit when calculating their retirement annuities even though a portion of their pension will be paid by each system.

CHANGES IN FUTURE PENSIONS

As of January 1, 2011 a new two-tier pension system took effect for public school employees. Current members of TRS, CTPF, IMRF, and other reciprocal systems (Tier I) are not affected by the changes. However, employees hired after January 1, 2011 are subject to Tier II regulations (Teachers' Retirement System, 2020). These changes are substantial. In fact, Tier II hires can expect significantly reduced retirement benefits than their Tier I counterparts.

Even more recently, the state added the Tier III plan, which lowers state pension costs. However, because of a plan provision that places new employees automatically in Tier III unless they take the initiative to request Tier II, some employees may make a retirement plan decision they may ultimately regret. Although the impact of the changes is a long way off for most new hires, an understanding of future retirement benefits is essential for long-term financial planning.

ADVISING EMPLOYEES

As you can see from our discussion, each of the retirement systems is somewhat complex. Administrators need to understand the basic provisions, especially related to Tier III after its implementation, in order to work with boards of education and employee groups. However, they also need to exercise caution when advising individual employees. Retirement system personnel have the knowledge necessary to calculate retirement annuities and are the only ones authorized to answer employee questions. Although it is appropriate to have preliminary discussions with employees about retirement, responsible administrators will always refer employees to their respective retirement systems for advice and any potential pension calculations.

PENSION UNCERTAINTY

At the moment, the pension system is not under the level of legislative scrutiny that it was a few years ago. However, a growing unfunded pension liability coupled with a lack of adequate state revenues may lead to increased interest by legislators to look for ways to scale back pension benefits. However, Illinois constitutional pension language appears to limit any legislative action that reduces benefits. A few years ago, the Illinois legislature and the governor approved a bill that would have scaled back pension benefits. In response, lawsuits were filed that challenged the legality of this legislation. Ultimately, the Illinois Supreme Court clarified that the constitution does not permit a reduction in pension benefits. What, if any, actions legislators and the governor will take in the future remain unclear.

OTHER EMPLOYEE RETIREMENT SAVINGS OPTIONS

In addition to the defined benefit retirement plans, most school districts will provide voluntary access to defined contribution plans in which employees may participate to supplement their pensions. These are individually owned investment accounts to which employees contribute a portion of their regular income. Since they are retirement accounts, most employees are not able to withdraw funds without a substantial tax penalty until they are 59 ½ years old. The three most well known options potentially available to K-12 public school employees are the regular 403(b), Roth 403(b), and 457 deferred compensation plans (Internal Revenue Service, 2023).

403(b)

The most widely offered defined contribution plan in Illinois public school districts is the 403(b), a tax deferred retirement plan. Offered through the school district, employees contribute pre-tax dollars to an investment account with a district authorized investment or annuity company through a payroll reduction agreement. The investment account earnings grow tax deferred until withdrawal (usually after retirement) but no sooner than age 59 ½ or as a result of separation of service at 55. Fund withdrawals are subject to the employee's regular income tax rate (Internal Revenue Service, 2023). Participants typically have several investment options through mutual funds companies or annuities issued by insurance companies. Employees for 2023 may contribute up to $22,500 of income or $30,000 if 50 or older (Internal Revenue Service, 2023).

Roth 403(b)

Another type of defined contribution plan, which became available is the Roth 403(b). Some school districts make it available to employees. The Roth is largely the same as the regular 403(b) with one important exception. Employees make after-tax contributions; however, all qualifying distributions are tax free. Depending upon their personal circumstances such as age and projected income tax level at retirement, participants need to weigh which type of 403(b) makes the most sense for their individual circumstances (Internal Revenue Service, 2023).

457 Deferred Compensation

A third type is the 457 Deferred Compensation plan, a tax deferred retirement savings vehicle very similar to the 403(b). Contribution levels are the same as the 403(b); however, one important consideration is that an employee may participate in both a 403(b) and a 457 simultaneously thereby doubling the amount they can invest. For example, teachers 50 years of age or older with sufficient income can invest up to $60,000 annually. A 457 also provides opportunities to withdraw funds penalty free prior to 59½ in certain situations (Internal Revenue Service, 2023).

Each of the three optional retirement savings plans offers the potential for employees to plan efficiently and effectively for retirement. However, similar to any investment, these are not without risk especially since they are often highly invested in the stock market. As of January 1, 2009, school districts assumed more additional responsibilities for 403(b) plans including providing information to employees and oversight for employee investments and fee assessments.

TRS SUPPLEMENTAL 457 DEFERRED SAVINGS PLAN (SSP)

As of January 2022, TRS members were eligible to participate in this new voluntary Supplemental 457 Deferred Savings Plan (Teachers' Retirement System, 2023). Members can contribute even if their school district does not offer a 457 option. The plan does not replace the current Tier I and II pension plans but rather provides members with an additional way to supplement their retirement saving.

This 457 is particularly advantageous for some TRS members. Since the plan is available throughout the state, employees who work in districts that do not offer a 457 option now have one available to them. Also, since it is a state-wide plan, it is portable meaning that even if you change school districts, you can continue contributing to your 457.

SUMMARY

In Chapter 8, we have examined four personnel-related areas including staffing patterns, compensation models, fringe benefits including healthcare options, and retirement planning. Each of these impacts the financial position of the district. School administrators must be well informed in each area if they are to be an efficient and effective school-level and district leaders.

Chapter 9

Financial Distress

Although many school districts are able to maintain a reasonable financial position by maximizing their regular sources of revenue, controlling expenditures, and utilizing long-term financial planning strategies, some school districts cannot. Even though they do their best to maintain a stable educational program with limited resources, ultimately many arrive at a point where sound fiscal management alone is just not enough. This is especially true for school districts under PTELL restrictions where revenues do not keep pace with escalating expenditures and non-capped district with relatively flat or even declining EVAs.. For those districts, school boards must find additional revenues and/or expenditure reductions, usually a daunting task.

The most realistic solution for school districts with eroding financial positions is to pass an operating fund tax increase. This requires school boards to ask district voters to increase property taxes through a referendum. All that is required is that a majority of registered voters in the school district vote "yes" for the referendum.

While some districts solve their immediate financial problems through referendums, others unfortunately fail referenda after referenda. As a result, these school boards have little or no choice but to watch their financial positions deteriorate to the point that the school district finds itself in a severe financial crisis. When school district finances reach the stage where no further staffing, program, or service cuts are realistic, the district finds itself teetering on the brink of financial crisis.

In this chapter, we will explore both of these scenarios: seeking additional property tax revenue through a referendum and the process legislated in Illinois to respond to imminent school district insolvency.

REFERENDUM CHALLENGES

Although a property tax increase is an effective revenue enhancement strategy, passing one is a substantial challenge. In today's anti-tax, and in particular, anti-property tax environment, school boards and administrators face an uphill battle to convince taxpayers to increase school funding. Recently, my wife and I went to dinner with some old friends, both of whom were retired. Since this was an election year, the conversation naturally turned to politics as we lamented the ongoing barrage of candidate commercials. At one point I asked them who they supported for office. Even I was surprised by the answer I received since I had always seen my friends as good supporters of education. One of them responded, "Anyone who won't raise my taxes." This experience reminded me that school administrators and board members can never afford to take educational support for granted. Rather, they must listen carefully to public opinion. Unfortunately, my friend's response is typical of how many of our constituents feel.

The reality for school board members and administrators is that winning public support for additional revenues will continue to be a significant challenge especially related to tax increases for operations. Typically, less than 40% succeed. However, in April 2023, 40% of referendum questions to raise school district tax rates, sell bonds, exceed PTELL, or establish a sales tax for school facilities were approved. (Illinois Association of School Boards, 2023). This in contrast to last year when the success rate was 50%. In any event, school district leaders need to understand the factors that contribute to continued public anti-tax sentiments if they plan to execute a successful referendum campaign.

FACTORS AFFECTING REFERENDUM SUCCESS

As school leaders plan for a referendum campaign, the ability to recognize the obstacles they will face is critical. A low key, non-publicized referendum approach will not likely succeed. Rather, referendum committees need to convince a wide variety of constituents, often with very different and strongly held positions, of the importance of a tax increase. This raises the question – What factors affect referendum campaigns?

Probably the most common factor is the general public's perception that taxes are too high. Strike up a conversation with your neighbors about taxes and, in particular, property taxes and I am sure you will hear a great deal of consternation. We see this sentiment echoed during local, state, and federal elections around, which politicians regularly ratchet up the anti-tax message.

An additional factor is the public's perception of the quality of education. Since at least the publication of A Nation at Risk in 1983 which described the perceived shortcomings of our public schools and placed substantial blame for perceived failing on both educators and our educational system, public education has been under national scrutiny. Again and again, we read about the lack of student achievement including declining student performance against international competition. We also hear education opponents arguing that adequate public school funding is already provided if only we used these resources properly. Often these discussions, which can be perceived as a partisan attack on public education, are driven by the media and centered on the need to set higher standards for teachers, administrators, and students. This intense media scrutiny and barrage of negatively-focused reports portray our educational system as broken.

Another reality is that we live in a society that is me-centered. Let me relate an experience, which illustrates my point. As superintendent, it was not usual for me to be confronted by groups of parents who employed high pressure tactics to demand special programs or services for their children, even if this meant that other children were negatively affected. One such event immediately comes to mind. A husband and wife, who considered themselves school-community activists, wanted their children's bus stop changed. Their two children had to walk less than a block in a quiet suburban neighborhood to catch the bus. They felt this was inconvenient, particularly in winter, and demanded that the stop be relocated in front of their home.

The business manager and I met with them to discuss their request. After reviewing all pertinent data, we explained to them that we could not move the stop since it would mean a section of the route would have to be revised, which would add additional route time. We also pointed out that other children would be inconvenienced by having to walk over from another street. Their response was that they did not care about the route length or other children. They paid taxes and were influential PTA members and their children should be accommodated. When we did not make the change, they threatened to take the issue to the school board and PTA. Over the next few years, they continued to create ongoing controversy using this event to stir others issues.

The important lesson here is not the actual decision made, but the fact that administrators regularly deal with some individuals who are "me" focused, rather than willing to consider the greater good. Similar to these parents, when presented with a tax increase request, a significant portion of the population may ask – "What is best for me?" A stumbling block in any referendum campaign is attempting to convince individuals who will not benefit directly from the tax increase that it is in the best interest of the community even if it means that they pay higher property taxes. What is somewhat ironic in my example above is that these parents would actually be referendum supporters since their children would personally benefit from increased school district revenue. However, what might their position be in a few years after their children are grown?

Beside parent special interest groups, referendum planners must research community demographics. Traditionally, those who benefit from a referendum such as parents and employees will vote "yes" at a higher rate than others. However, referendum planners need to keep in mind that not all parents will be supporters. What is important to remember is that communities are primarily composed of individuals who have little interest in the day-to-day activities of the school.

One such group is taxpayers who either have no children or whose children no longer attend district schools. In one district where I served as an administrator, this group represented almost 80% of eligible voters.

By way of example, let me relate one more story. Several years ago, I had a wealthy friend who I would describe as reasonably community-minded. He owned a very successful business. His children had all been "school stars" both academically and athletically. He had nothing but good things to say about the local school system, which his children attended.

One day, after they graduated, our school district went to referendum. As an educator, I was naturally a supporter and assumed from his past history that he would be too. At a neighborhood get-together, the referendum came up. When I said that I was voting for it, I remember being surprised when he said that he would not. For him, money was not an issue. His children had benefited from their educations, and he generally was a positive person. What he next said was instructive. He noted that he had done his share by supporting past referenda and paying substantial property taxes over the years. Now he said it was someone else's turn since his family would not longer benefit from any tax increase.

What is important to consider from these real life examples is that they highlight the importance of conducting a comprehensive referendum campaign. From my experience, the days of counting on a majority of the community to vote for increased school funding just because the school board supports it or because it is the right thing to do are gone. Today, referendum success is largely linked to winning over more than the traditional "yes" voters.

CONDUCTING A SUCCESSFUL REFERENDUM CAMPAIGN

A referendum is really more of a political than an educational process for which administrators are often unprepared and/or ill-equipped. Many will need the assistance of attorneys and financial consultants to guide them through the referendum process because they may be unfamiliar with all the legal requirements including adopting a referendum question. Some referendum committees even hire consultants to assist them in the political process. What is probably most useful for you to understand is how to conduct a comprehensive referendum campaign, which will be discussed in this section. However, before we do let's distinguish between the two most common types of referendums: building bonds and operating rate.

Building Bond Referendum

A building bond referendum is primarily facilities-focused. Schools boards, who want to renovate schools, build additions, or construct new schools, can ask the local taxpayers for a temporary tax increase to generate a specific dollar amount to use for specified improvements. A building referendum is the preferred option when a school district lacks sufficient operating revenue or reserves to fund a major project. For example, if a school board wants to build a new elementary school but needs an additional $20M, the school board would ask the taxpayers for the authority to sell bonds through a referendum. If more than fifty percent of the voters approve, the school board is allowed to tax property owners for the $20M.

Once a referendum is approved by the voters, the school board can sell building bonds to pay for the project. Usually building bonds are paid back over a period of at least 15 years. Bond holders receive repayment of their principal with interest over some specified period of time from annual property tax proceeds.

One additional point is worth noting. Building referenda, which are "brick and mortar" projects, historically succeed at a higher rate than requests for operating fund tax increases. During the April 2023 election, this figure was 50% (Illinois Association of School Boards, 2023).

Operating Referendum

The second type of referendum is designed to increase property taxes permanently for school district operations. Unlike a building referendum with a specified focus, school districts have greater latitude to choose how to use additional tax revenues generated through an operating fund referendum. Most often, these new revenues support educational programs and services. However, before discussing this type of referendum, an important consideration is to recognize the differences in referendum requests between tax-capped and non-tax capped school districts.

TAX-CAPPED (PTELL) SCHOOL DISTRICTS

According to the Illinois Department of Revenue, PTELL school districts are allowed to seek voter approval to increase property taxes. However, because of recent changes in the law, formulating a referendum question in tax capped counties has become more complex. Sections 18-120 and 18-125 of the Property Tax Code identify four types of referendum questions (Illinois Department of Revenue, 2023b). These include:
- Increasing the extension limit;
- Increasing the limiting rate;
- Levying for a new tax rate; and,
- Increasing the debt extension service base.

Since these can be confusing, school districts will often employ financial consultants in order to select the most advantageous option.

NON-TAX CAPPED SCHOOL DISTRICTS

In non-tax capped school districts, the referendum process has remained essentially the same as in the recent past. When a school board seeks a property tax increase through a referendum, the district asks taxpayers to approve an increase in the tax rate of a specific fund.

The school board may levy the requested rate against the total taxable district EAV as long as the requested tax rate increase does not exceed the state maximum for a particular fund.

To illustrate this, let's consider an example. Here are our assumptions.

- The school district is asking to increase its tax rate for the Education Fund by fifty cents from the current $1.00 to $1.50.
- The overall district EAV is $100M.
- The district plans to levy the full fifty cent increase the first year.

Although the example simplifies the factors and does not include some provisions that school district leaders would normally consider if they were conducting an actual referendum, it does demonstrate the basic process.

To calculate the approximate effect of tax increase on increased school district revenues in the Education Fund, you simply apply the property tax calculation discussed in Chapter 2:

- EAV/100 X Tax Rate Increase = Additional Property Taxes
- 1,000,000 ($100M/100) X 0.50 = $500,000

If you are considering a property tax increase through a referendum, remember that you will want to seek professional expertise from an attorney or financial consultant to ensure that you meet all legal requirements.

PASSING A REFERENDUM

Given the complexity of passing a referendum, school boards and administrators must develop a comprehensive referendum campaign plan built around a network of multiple stakeholders. Complicating any referendum, though, are state laws, which disallow the use of school district dollars to fund the referendum campaign as well as restrictions on when and how school board members and district employees may promote the referendum (Braun, 2022). Consequently, "selling" the referendum falls to a large extent on local residents who must not only lead the process but work many hours. Clearly, school leaders must educate the community about the district's financial needs if they are to mobilize community support.

A solid referendum campaign has its roots at the school board, staff, and community levels. When the school district administration determines that the additional tax revenues are essential in maintaining current programs and services, educating the school board, employees, and local residents as soon as possible is a priority. A lack of understanding about why additional tax revenues are needed usually translates into a lackluster referendum campaign and, subsequently, a failed effort.

One key to success is school board support. Often, some voters look to board members for guidance. District administrators must convince school board members that a referendum is imperative. Without the support of all seven school board members, winning a referendum becomes even more difficult.

Since referendum success rests to a large degree on the comprehensiveness of the referendum process, a key question to consider is – What are the stages in a successful referendum campaign?

To illustrate how a school district might design a successful referendum campaign, let's consider one employed by a suburban Chicago school district which passed an operating fund increase after failing a prior referendum (Kersten & Armour, 2004).

Phase 1. Building Support

Whether you have failed a previous referendum or are initiating your first in several years, a critical step is getting your message out early through school-community education. Although school district administrators may use a variety of strategies to accomplish this, all include identifying key local leaders and invested stakeholder groups. A successful approach used by our sample school district administrators and school board members was to conduct a series of reflection meetings for community leaders, parents, and district employees several months before the actual referendum day.

These sessions served a variety of purposes including:

- Assessing why the prior referendum failed;
- Identifying potential referendum supporters; and,
- Identifying referendum leadership team members who could direct the campaign.

From these sessions, a core group of motivated, knowledgeable leaders emerged who formed the heart of the community-based referendum team.

Phase 2. Pre-Referendum Campaign

After building an initial support base, the referendum process entered the pre-referendum campaign phase. At this point, since the school board had not yet officially initiated a referendum, district administrators had the latitude to educate as many residents and staff members as possible about the school district's financial needs. It was during this critical phase that much of the referendum groundwork was laid including the development of a comprehensive referendum campaign plan. It is important to remember that once a school board votes to place a referendum on the ballot, legal restrictions limit school board and employee involvement. However, it is also important to remember that school board members do not lose their rights as citizens and can serve in an individual capacity on the referendum committee.

During this stage, a critical step was selecting a referendum leadership team, which was responsible for developing the actual referendum campaign plan. Since this was pre-referendum, the superintendent and other district administrators were actively involved in the planning process.

As is typical of most successful referenda, the leadership team organized the campaign around a committee structure. Although the number, type, and scope of committees may vary from school district to school district, I have identified below those employed by the case study district.

Voter Registration. As noted earlier, a key to a successful referendum campaign requires getting out the "yes" vote. A good first step is taking every opportunity to ensure that the supporters are registered to vote. Strategies included:

- Initially contacting the county for a list of registered voters;
- Mounting a voter registration campaign;
- Sending information to unregistered voters about registration procedures and district needs;
- Distributing information on absentee voting;
- Targeting certain age groups such as those 18 to 25 years of age who might not otherwise vote;
- Consciously establishing voter registration stations wherever and whenever possible. Through the county, volunteers can be trained as official registrars and school and community events can be turn into voter registration opportunities; and,
- Confirming voter registrations with the county just prior to the voter registration deadline.

The referendum leadership team used these voter registration activities to increase the likelihood of reaching the "yes" voters.

Public Relations. The leadership team also recognized the value of tapping into local community residents with public relations experience to serve on the public relations committee which was charged with:

- Creating multiple publicity pieces ranging from informational letters to brochures to yard signs; even producing a video;
- Selecting a campaign theme with which residents identified;
- Preparing logos, response literature, buttons, and other forms of communication targeted to specific age and special interest groups; and,
- Serving as a resource to other referendum committees.

The public relations committee was invaluable in getting the referendum message out to voters.

Outreach. School districts are becoming increasingly diverse. As a result, successful referendum campaigns target district diversity whether related to specific age groups or special populations. This district's outreach committee planned specific activities to reach these unique groups. In addition, another major responsibility of the outreach committee was canvassing voters, which will be discussed later.

Data and Technology. Today more than ever, technology can be utilized to generate information and create access to the general public. An important committee to include in the referendum planning process is data and technology. Any referendum effort requires gathering large amounts of data about the district and potential voters. Our sample school district's data and technology committee increased the efficiency of the campaign by:

- Synthesizing and analyzing election and voter data;
- Gathering and analyzing voter information; and,
- Providing technical assistance to other committees.

Fundraising. As noted earlier, state law prohibits school districts from using district funds to finance a referendum campaign. This raises the question – who will pay for such items as informational materials, advertising, supplies, and phone calls? The answer is the referendum committee. As a result, in our sample district, a fundraising committee composed of volunteers with fundraising interest and, in some instances, experience raised adequate dollars to fund all planned activities. It is important to remember that Illinois political disclosure requirements apply to the referendum committee.

Phase 3: The Actual Campaign

After the Board of Education officially authorized the referendum, the actual campaign began. At this point, the referendum plan was in place. The school district administration had explained the financial position of the district. Community members were well aware that a referendum was imminent. The stage was now set for the actual formal campaign to begin.

It is important to note that a school board should not initiate a referendum sooner than three months before election day. If you begin a formal referendum campaign too early, you might have difficulty maintaining a high level of positive momentum while also increasing the risk of organized opposition.

However, once the referendum is certified, much needs to be accomplished. Some good advice I once received from an experienced superintendent who passed many referendums can be summed up in three simple statements:

- Identify the "yes" voters;
- Forget the "no" voters; and,
- Win over the "maybe" voters.

This is how every campaign from the presidency to a school referendum is won.

Given these three focuses, the case study district Outreach Committee employed a sophisticated voter canvassing process. As the superintendent told me later, this was probably the most critical part of the political process because here was where they actually identified, primarily through personal contact, the perceived yes, no, and maybe voters. The canvass activities of the oversight committee included:

- Contacting as many eligible voters as possible to determine their voting inclination;
- Conducting a door-to-door canvass of registered voters who were thought to be supporters but had not been reached by phone;
- Personalizing the message by encouraging supporters to contact neighbors and friends; and,
- Reminding voters about the referendum through cards and letters from respected community members just before election day.

Phase 4: Election Day

After months of hard work, referendum day finally arrived, but the work of the committee was not yet complete. On this day, when anticipation and excitement built, it was important to remember that the focus of the referendum campaign was to get out the "yes" vote. Consequently, every effort was made to use these last few hours to meet this goal. Several strategic ways the referendum committee used their volunteers on election day included:

- Designating poll watchers who not only recorded those who voted but also identified potential "yes" voters who had not yet voted so they could be contacted. Poll watchers also monitored the fairness of the election, challenged negative comments made to voters from election judges, observed vote counting, and reported election results to the referendum committee after votes were tallied;
- Placing volunteers outside polling places to distribute literature and encourage a positive vote;
- Designating phone personnel to receive calls from poll watchers and assist with communication among other committee members;
- Using "runners" who walked the precincts reminding supporters to vote and later in the day contacting "yes" voters who had not yet voted;
- Manning election central to coordinate the day's efforts; and,
- Establishing a meeting spot for all election volunteers to gather to tally unofficial election results and later that evening host a victory party, which they did!

Nothing is more satisfying to school district stakeholders than the feelings associated with a referendum victory. All the planning and hard work has paid off. The school district will now be financially sound for years to come. Everyone can turn their attention back to their real priority – providing an outstanding education for district children.

However, for other school districts, continued referendum failures may ultimately lead to financial insolvency. This raises an important question – What happens when a school district's financial position deteriorates to the point that it is on the verge of insolvency?

SCHOOL DISTRICT INSOLVENCY

Although most school districts use a combination of revenue enhancements and expenditure controls to maintain financial viability, a few cannot escape financial crisis. These school districts usually have explored multiple options to increase revenues and failed several operating fund referendums. They have also "cut" educational programs and services to the point where only the most basic educational programs and services are offered. In addition, they have exhausted almost all their reserves. When school districts arrive at this point and are on the brink of insolvency, outside intervention becomes a reality.

During the 1990s when a few school districts began to reach the insolvency stage, the Illinois State Board of Education (ISBE) in cooperation with the Illinois Legislature passed legislation entitled School District Financial Assistance which was designed to help school districts resolve their financial crises (105ILCS 5/1B-1 to 1B-22). As of FY22, two school districts are designated by ISBE as under formal Financial Oversight. These include East St. Louis School District 189 and North Chicago School District 187 (Illinois State Board of Education, 2023f).

FINANCIAL OVERSIGHT PROCESS

When school districts near the point of insolvency, their school boards may ask ISBE to certify them in Financial Distress (105ILCS 5/1A-8). When school boards make this request, they are aware that they are relinquishing a significant portion of their decision-making authority for expenditures. They also become subject to mandated ISBE intervention.

Financial Difficulty

The first level of state intervention is Financial Difficulty. These are school districts designated by ISBE as "in financial difficulty," that is, nearing insolvency. ISBE requires these districts to develop, adopt, and submit a financial plan within 45 days of certification. They also are required to report regularly to the State Board of Education and provide reports documenting such items as budget data, financial statements, and other information as requested by ISBE (Braun, 2022). Recently, Streator School District 44 was at this level but has now emerged (Illinois State Board of Education, 2022f). School districts designated in Financial Difficulty unable to achieve solvency move to the next level, Financial Oversight.

Financial Oversight

The second level of state intervention is the financial Oversight process. The school district may voluntarily request that ISBE designate a Financial Oversight Panel (FOP) or the State Board may appoint one. The FOP is composed of five board members appointed by the state superintendent of schools. Two must be residents. None can be school board members, employees, or others with a financial interest in the district. Members are selected on the basis of experience and knowledge of financial management, especially public education.

The FOP's primary purpose is to exercise financial control of the district by taking such actions as employing executive management administrators such as a Chief Executive Officer, Chief Education Officer, Chief Financial Officer, Superintendent, Chief School Business Official; approving expenditures and the annual budget; approving contracts; and negotiating collective bargaining agreements. The FOP may engage in short-term borrowing with provisions but may not sell bonds. The goal of the FOP is to provide school districts with technical assistance and guidance to return the district to financial solvency (Illinois State Board of Education, 2023f).

As you might imagine, the shifting of authority for all financial decisions to the FOP can create some management and political issues especially if the school board and FOP do not work collaboratively together. However, because of the need to address tough financial decisions, the FOP was purposely designed to operate independent of the school board and voting public.

Dissolving the Financial Oversight

Since this legislation was initially approved, several school districts have functioned under ISBE Financial Oversight. Some school districts were ultimately dissolved or annexed to neighboring school districts while in others oversight was discontinued. Several school districts including Round Lake Area School District 116, Cairo Unit District 1, Cahokia CUSD 187, Harrisburg CUSD 3, Venice Community School District 3, Hazel Crest Unit School District 152.5, Proviso Township High School District 209, and Streator Elementary School District 44 have successfully emerged from oversight. Each ultimately earned ISBE's "Financial Recognition" status. (Illinois State Board of Education, 2023f).

A FOP may be abolished in as little as three years, but not more than ten. The decision to abolish an FOP is tied to the progress the school district makes toward achieving financial stability including meeting its financial plan goals and objectives.

SUMMARY

In Chapter 9, we examined both how school districts use the referendum process to generate much needed school district revenues as well as the Illinois financial oversight process defined in law for those school districts who are near insolvency. These two scenarios illustrate the importance of financial planning along with the impact of wide variances in school funding throughout Illinois.

Chapter 10

Emerging Issues in Illinois School Finance

As I noted in the financial planning chapter, school administrators must accept the reality that as they plan for the future, they must be prepared for the unexpected. Because public education is so closely tied to the state legislative process and political realities, school administrators must pay close attention not only to what is happening at the state and national levels but also anticipate what issues might emerge in the near future. In this chapter, several important school finance issues which have or may have an impact on public education are discussed.

EQUITABLE FUNDING LEVELS

The wide variances in per pupil spending, which impact both the scope and quality of educational programs and services in Illinois public schools, is a real dilemma. The gap is large and may continue to grow. The Illinois State Board of Education (2023d) reported that Aviston SD 21 ranked at the bottom in operating expenditures per pupil, spending $6,503 per student. Ohio CHSD 505 was on the other end of the spectrum in the state with expenditures of $39,033 per child. Since the Illinois Constitution does not require equity, any solution to this problem lies with the legislative process. With the new state Evidence-Based Funding model, the plan is to gradually reduce these inequities moving forward. However, the issues of equity and adequacy are not likely to disappear quickly. These discrepancies in funding and access to education opportunities will likely continue to be a state-wide issue for some time.

SCHOOL FUNDING REFORM

Back in the early 1990s, a major finance topic which regularly dominated the school finance reform discussion was imposing a tax cap on property. As an assistant superintendent at the time, I, similar to many of my administrative colleagues, worried each time the state legislature met because we feared that something onerous would emerge from the legislative session. However, we knew that year in and year out, various governors had appointed finance commissions whose work ultimately resulted in no change or at best some tinkering with funding formulas. We learned that as any sweeping changes were unlikely to occur.

This was the prevalent feeling among many of my administrative colleagues as the issue of tax caps surfaced once again. We assumed that by the end of the legislative session clearer heads would ultimately prevail and that legislators would never be able to summon the votes necessary to pass tax cap legislation. In the recent past, there had been ongoing rhetoric about tax caps but no actual action. We believed that our local political leaders would ultimately recognize the negative impact tax caps would have on the financial viability of property tax dependent school districts. However, to our surprise, we suddenly found ourselves with a tax cap as a result of a political compromise. This action changed forever how many of us view the legislative process.

In recent years other school finance reform initiatives have occupied the political agenda. One, which continues to receive substantial attention, is the property tax swap. Under this scenario, Illinois property taxes would be reduced and replaced with an increase in the level of state income taxes. On the surface, this makes a great deal of sense to the general public who as we have seen are generally anti-property taxes. To the average person it makes more sense to fund schools through increased income tax rates since those with higher incomes would shoulder a much greater burden for school funding.

Proponents argue that a state income tax approach would generate more revenue for schools which could be distributed to school districts more equitably thereby reducing the wide variances among school districts dollars spent per student. They point out that basing the funding system on income versus property ownership would help ensure equitable educational programs and services since the revenues district receive would not be as dependent on local property wealth.

Opponents counter that once school funding shifts from the property tax which is essential free of the state political process and a highly reliable source of school district revenue to an income tax based system, education funding will be reduced in property wealthy districts because the revenues lost will not be replaced dollar for dollar under the new funding model. Rather, the stability of the property tax as a source of revenue would be replaced by an annual state budgeting process which would place a greater percentage of school revenues into a political-based legislative process. Opponents caution that many school districts would actually experience a reduction in school district revenues.

As school funding reform initiatives such as the tax swap or even state-mandated property tax reductions are proposed, local school administrators, school board members, and other stakeholders would be wise to ensure that they are informed on the issues and prepared to articulate their positions through the political process.

TAX CAP AND INFLATION

For many years, we have lived in an era marked by low inflation rates. As discussed in Chapter 5, historically the annual rate of inflation has remained below the maximum tax cap level of 5%. However, for the past two yeas, the CPI has exceeded the maximum. If this high inflation level continues, the entire conversation around issues, such as balancing the budget and collective bargaining, is poised to change. In fact, some school districts are already facing increased salary and other costs due to the impact of inflation.

BUSINESS PROPERTY TAX APPEALS

In the district where I was superintendent, it was common for large business property owners to regularly appeal their property tax assessments. In many instances, individual school districts found themselves at a severe disadvantage when fighting these appeals to preserve their tax bases. As a result, school districts and other local governmental units throughout the suburban Chicago area recognized the mutual benefits of banding together to collaborate in their fight to reduce the effects of appeals filed within the property tax appeal board. Business leaders quickly learned that they could either use the legal process available to them to win a property assessment reduction or negotiate a compromise settlement with the taxing bodies.

In our school district, we regularly experienced business property tax assessment reductions of as much as a $1,000,000, some of which was for past years since the time required processing the appeals generally extended out several years. Since our school district was tax capped and tax rates usually below the maximums, we could recoup the loss of these business property taxes in future years by increasing the property taxes of other taxpayers. However, we experienced real property tax revenue losses for prior years because these dollars were rebated without an option to recover them. In December 2021, Public Law 102-0519 passed. It allows school districts to re-coup the cost of PTAB refunds through a recapture levy (Robbins Schwartz, 2021).

School administrators and subsequently school boards need to be vigilant in not only fighting business property tax appeals but also staying informed on ongoing changes in the legal process. In fact, local governmental consortiums need to monitor all aspects of the business tax appeal process, lobby legislators to increase school district standing in the appeals process, and even propose new legislative remedies. Since businesses will continue to seek new and even creative approaches to reduce their property taxes, this issue will remain an ongoing concern in the future.

FUNDING SHORTFALLS

Traditionally, each spring, state funding shortfalls tend to dominate legislative discussions about school funding. For FY23, this topic has not disappeared but received less attention as the governor has made school funding a legislative priority. However, as Illinois recovers from the pandemic, it is important to recognize that the topic of state funding shortfalls may again be a more visible concern.

STAFFING SHORTAGES

School districts across the state are feeling the pressures of teacher and support staff shortages. In addition to the educational ramifications, these shortages are driving up salary and benefit costs as school districts negotiate collective bargaining agreements and look to provide additional of improved benefits to enhance employee recruitment. This issue is likely to be a problem for some time.

STATE LEGISLATIVE LEADERSHIP

For many years, legislative action and non-action were reasonably predictable as speakers in both the Senate and especially the House exercised strong control over the movement of legislation. Now that this leadership has changed and appears more open to additional bills reaching the congressional floor, this may have an impact on legislative action. School leaders should monitor this closely.

PENSION UNDER-FUNDING

An ongoing concern throughout the state is the under-funding of the Teacher Retirement System. For decades, the state has failed to fully fund its required pension obligation thereby weakening TRS's long-term financial stability. Although the contribution rates of pension system participants and more recently school boards have increased, these alone are not sufficient to fully fund pension liabilities. Because of the lack of full state TRS funding and increasing pension obligations related to retiree longevity, a more permanent solution to the under-funding problem must be found.

During recent years, the Illinois Legislature has changed pension benefits for new public school employees. On an ongoing basis, the legislature is actively considering additional ways to reduce pension benefits for current and even retired employees. Because of Illinois Constitution provisions, their options are limited.

At the moment, pension reform is not at the top of the political conversations. Also, the governor and legislators are increasing Illinois funding for pensions beyond the annual required minimum. The question is whether this push to more fully fund the pensions system is a one year action or is the beginning of a strategy to increase pension systems stability.

PACE OF LEGISLATIVE ACTION

Illinois has a long tradition of broad-based involvement in legislative decision-making. Historically, the two political parties have taken different positions on many legislative issues. This tended to stir considerable public debate on major legislative initiatives. As part of this process, the public, especially those most affected by the legislation, were brought into the debate.

How quickly times have changed! Today, legislators and the governor are from the same political party. They have the authority to pass legislation as they deem appropriate. Even with this shift, school boards, administrators, and employees may or may not have increased influence on issues that affect them directly. They must monitor legislative action and be prepared to voice their opinions quickly and forcefully.

SUMMARY

In this chapter, we have examined several imminent issues in Illinois school finance. This list is far from complete. What is important to remember is that school leaders must not only focus on the day-to-day operations of their school districts, but also maintain a keen awareness of both immediate and potential school finance issues.

Closing Thoughts

In this book, I have discussed the major topics in Illinois school finance that impact both sides of the school finance equation: revenues and expenditures. Hopefully, I have met the 7-Eleven test by making school finance more understandable for a wide audience of interested stakeholders, including those who are employed or have a vested interest in public education. In order to provide our children with a world class education that will allow them to lead productive and self-satisfying lives, we must all share responsibility for fully funding our system of public education. An important first step is to understand the basics of school funding in Illinois.

References

Alexander, K., & Alexander, M. D. (2005). American public school law (6th ed.). Belmont, CA: Thompson Learning, Inc.

Benson, C. M. (2006). Tax increment financing. Journal of School Business Management. *18*(2), 11-17.

Beyer, B. M., & Johnson, E. S. (2005). Special programs & services in schools: Creating options, meeting needs. Lancaster, PA: Pro Active Publications.

Braun, B. A. (2022). Illinois school law survey (17th ed.). Springfield, IL: Illinois Association of School Boards.

Brimley, V, & Garfield, R. (2004). Financing education in a climate of change (8th ed.). Boston, MA: Allyn and Bacon.

Chicago Teacher Pension Fund. (20223). Member information. Retrieved May 3, 2023 from http://ctpf.org/general_info/publications.htm

Fix the Formula. (2017). Evidence-based model (EBM) – Fix the formula Illinois. Retrieved September 18, 2017 from http://fundingilfuture.org/wp-content/uploads/2017/05/Full-EBM-FAQ-042517.pdf

Guthrie, J. W. (Ed.). (2003). Encyclopedia of education (2nd ed.). New York, NY: Macmillan Reference USA.

HealthCare.gov. (2023). Health deductible health plans (HDHPs) & health savings accounts (HSAs). Retrieved April 20, 2022 from https://www.healthcare.gov/high-deductible-health-plan/hdhp-hsa-information/

Hennessy, E. (2023). Bond basics, Aurora University Presentation, IL: Raymond James & Associates.

Hennessy, E., Connor, R. R., & Prombo, M. J. (2014). Won't you be my neighbor?

Herman, E. & Kownacki, M. (2008). Cook County board approves Houlihan's proposal to reduce assessment levels. Available from: http://www.cookcountyassessor.com/info/news/inthenews01.asp?ID=193

Houlihan, J. M. (2009). Cook county assessor. Retrieved July 6, 2009 from www.cookcounty assessor.com/1025.aspx

Illinois Association of School Administrators. (2017). The evidence-based model for school funding. Retrieved October 1, 2017 from https:///www.iasaedu.org/cms/lib/IL01923163/Centricity/Domain/4/SB1947%20-%2026%20elements%20included.pdf

Illinois Association of School Boards (2023). IASB News: November '22 referendum results. Retrieved from https://www.iasb.com/news-listing/2023/april-2023-news/mixed-outcomes-in-april-%E2%80%9823-referendum-results/

Illinois Association of School Boards. (2006). Where does the lottery money go? {Brochure}. Springfield, IL: Author.

Illinois Department of Revenue. (2023a). Property Tax Extension Limitation Law PTELL. Retrieved April 2, 2023 from https://tax.illinois.gov/localgovernments/property/ptell.html

Illinois Department of Revenue. (2023b). Personal property replacement tax. Retrieved March 28, 2023 from https://www2.illinois.gov/rev/localgovernments/Pages/replacement.aspx

Illinois Department of Revenue. (2023c). The Illinois property tax system. Retrieved March 22, 2023 from https://tax.illinois.gov/content/dam/soi/en/web/tax/research/publications/documents/localgovernment/ptax-1004.pdf

Illinois Department of Revenue. (2023d). 2021 Cook County Final Multiplier Announced, Retrieved March 22, 2023 from https://tax.illinois.gov/research/news/2021-cook-county-final-multiplier-announced.html

Illinois Department of Revenue. (2022e). Property Tax Limitation Law. Retrieved April 10, 2023 from https://www2.illinois.gov/rev/research/publications/Documents/localgovernment/ptax1080.pdf

Illinois Municipal Retirement Fund. (2023). Your benefits under IMRF. Author. Available from: http://www.imrf.org

Illinois State Board of Education. (2022a). 2021 annual report. Available from https://www.isbe.net/Documents/2021AnnualReport.pdf#search=2022%20annual%20report

Illinois State Board of Education. (2023b). Evidenced-based funding basics: A practical guide for district administrators. Retrieved March 28, 2023 from https://www.isbe.net/Documents/EBF-Basics-Fall-2020.pdf

Illinois State Board of Education. (2023c). General State Aid. Author. Available from: https://www.isbe.net/Documents/gas_overview.pdf

Illinois State Board of Education. (2021d). School business services. Author. Available from: https://www.isbe.net/Pages/Operating-Expense-Per-Pupil.aspx

Illinois State Board of Education. (2023e). School district financial profile. Author. Available from: http://www.isbe.net/Pages/School-District-Financial-Profile.aspx

Illinois State Board of Education. (2023f). Financial oversight panels and school finance authorities. Retrieved April 1, 2023 from https://www.isbe.net/Pages/Financial-Oversight-Panels-and-School-Finance-Authorities.aspx

Illinois Tax Increment Association. (2023). ITIFA Website. Author. Available from: http://www.illinois-tif.com

Illinois Teacher Retirement System. (2023). Teachers' Retirement System. Author.
Available from: http://www.trsil.org

Internal Revenue Service. (2023). IRS Website. Available from www/irs.gov

Kaiser Family Foundation. (2022). 2021 Employer health benefits survey.
Retrieved April 1, 2022 from: https://www.kff.org/health-costs/report/2021-employer-health-benefits-survey/

Kersten, T. A. (2006). State financial oversight: An option for insolvent school districts.
Journal of School Business Management, *18*(2), 8-12.

Kersten, T. A. (2008). Understanding new growth under the Illinois property tax extension
limitation law (PTELL). Journal of School Business Management, *20*(1), p. 15-21.

Kersten, T. A., & Armour, N. (2004). Education fund rate increase: You can pass it.
Journal of School Business Management, *16*(2), 36-43.

Kersten, T. A., & Dada, M. (2005). Skyrocketing healthcare costs: Is there a cure? The
Journal of School Business Management, *17*(1), 17-24.

Kersten, T. A., & Diaz, M. A. (2021). School district benefits: What are leaders thinking
about today? The Journal of School Business Management, *33*(1), 13-16.

National Institute of Health (2023). National Institute of Health, 2023 Flexible spending
accounts – New 2023 limits for the HCFSA. Retrieved April 20, 2023 from
https://hr.nih.gov/about/news/benefits-newsletter/2022/12/flexible-spending-accounts-program-new-2023-limits-hcfsa-and

Our Lady of Angels Fire Memorial. (2008). Our Lady of Angels (OLA) school fire
December 1, 1958. Author. Available from: http://www.olafire.com/OtherFacts.asp

Robbins Schwartz, (2021). Department of Revenue guidance concludes PTAB refund
recapture applies to PTELL and Non-PTELL districts. Author. Available from:
https://www.rsnlt.com/news/law-alerts/2021/12/03/department-of-revenue-guidance-concludes-ptab-refund-recapture-applies-to-ptell-and-non-ptell-districts/#:~:text=The%20Illinois%20Department%20of%20Revenue%20recently%20issued%20a,for%20the%20upcoming%20December%202021%20property%20tax%20levies.

State of Illinois (2023). Retirement System Reciprocal Act. Available from:
https://www.srs.illinois.gov/PDFILES/brochures/recip.pdf

Stevenson High School Foundation. (2023). Donor impact and annual report: 2017-2018.
Available from: https://www.stevensonfoundation.org/who-we-are

The Commonwealth Fund. (2022). Essential facts about drug pricing reform: Inflation
rebate for drug companies. Retrieved April 7, 2022 from
https://www.commonwealthfund.org/publications/explainer/2021/jun/inflation-rebate-penalty-drug-companies

NiceRx (2023). The US prescription drug report 2021. Retrieved April 21, 2023 from
https://www.nicerx.com/prescription-drug-report-2021/

U. S. Office of Special of Education. (2023). History: A Twenty---Five Years of Progress in Educating Children with Disabilities Through IDEA. Author. Available from: https://sites.ed.gov/idea/files/idea-history.pdf

White, J. (2007). Illinois handbook of government 2007-2008. Springfield, IL: Illinois Secretary of State.

Yudof, M. G., Kirp, D. L., & Levin, B. (1992). Educational policy and the law (3rd ed.). St. Paul, MN: West Publishing Company.

Index